JOHN FURNISS

THREE MEN
UP A
MOUNTAIN

Memories of youthful climbing adventures
in Britain and Europe

JOHN FURNISS

THREE MEN
UP A
MOUNTAIN

Memories of youthful climbing adventures
in Britain and Europe

MEREO
Cirencester

Mereo Books

1A The Wool Market Dyer Street Cirencester Gloucestershire GL7 2PR
An imprint of Memoirs Publishing www.mereobooks.com

Three men up a mountain: 978-1-86151-637-4

First published in Great Britain in 2016
by Mereo Books, an imprint of Memoirs Publishing

The address for Memoirs Publishing Group Limited can be found at
www.memoirspublishing.com

The Memoirs Publishing Group Ltd Reg. No. 7834348

The Memoirs Publishing Group supports both The Forest Stewardship Council®
(FSC®) and the PEFC® leading international forest-certification organisations.
Our books carrying both the FSC label and the PEFC® and are printed on FSC®-
certified paper. FSC® is the only forest-certification scheme supported by the
leading environmental organisations including Greenpeace. Our paper procurement
policy can be found at www.memoirspublishing.com/environment

Typeset in 11/17pt Century Schoolbook
by Wiltshire Associates Publisher Services Ltd. Printed and bound in Great Britain
by Printondemand-Worldwide, Peterborough PE2 6XD

To my dear wife Marilyn and our lovely daughters
Laura and Gemma. This will save you having to listen to my
stories over and over again!

My thanks to Chris Newton of Memoirs for all
his hard work and advice on the text.

CONTENTS

Introduction

INTRODUCTION

Most of the time there were three of us. Sometimes there were only two and sometimes there were four, but usually there were three.

Three is a good number technically for climbing. There was another good reason for having a team of three; it meant that we always had a majority for decision making, unless of course there were three entirely different views!

There was also more than one mountain. There were in fact 39 mountains which we climbed during the decade that these stories relate to (the Sixties). Many of these mountains were climbed numerous times and we made 95 ascents in all, totalling more than 13 times the height of Mount Everest.

In the beginning our mountain climbing activities were purely an adventurous outdoor pursuit. However in time, especially as a very long undergraduate course began to take its toll, they started to provide a much needed safety-valve and a means to recharge our batteries.

This then is the story of all these stories about mountains and the men who climbed them.

CHAPTER ONE

1960
THE FIRST ASCENT

It all started as part of a publicity exercise for the Boy Scouts of Northampton. All the Scout troops in the town were invited to organise different events during the first weekend of May 1960 which would demonstrate to the public the wide range of skills and exciting activities that Scouting had to offer. The Senior Scout section of the 40th Northampton (the Grammar School Troop) had decided that we would travel to Wales and climb Snowdon. This was going to be a good challenge, as none of us had ever climbed a mountain before – there weren't too many of them in Northamptonshire!

We were all sixteen-year-olds apart from our long-suffering scoutmaster, Skip M, who was also a maths teacher at our school and whose age was unknown to us. The plan was to travel to Wales in a minibus on the Friday, camp that night, then tackle Snowdon on the Saturday morning.

Most of the journey was spent travelling along the A5, which took us north of Birmingham. The excitement started to become palpable once we had passed through Llangollen – in Wales at last! Once through Capel Curig the scenery started to have a distinctly mountainous flavour. We headed down the A4086 towards the Llanberis Pass, where we were going to camp in the car park near to the Gorphwysfa Hotel. This was ideally placed at the beginning of the Pyg Track which would lead us to the Snowdon Horseshoe the next morning.

The party consisted of seven of us Senior Scouts and Skip M, who was going to sleep in a small hike tent. The rest of us were going to sleep in a newly-acquired Icelandic mountain tent. A reasonable size to sleep 7-8 people, it was round and resembled a Mongolian yurt. It had a sewn-in groundsheet and a central pole. There were no windows and access was obtained by crawling through a sleeve. This was not very practical, we discovered, and it was mutually agreed that we should take our boots off before wriggling inside.

We chose a flat, if rather boggy, patch of ground to pitch the tent on. We reasoned that it should be soft to lie on and the sewn-in groundsheet would stop any mud leaking into the tent. We then laid out our sleeping bags radially around the pole, foot ends towards the centre.

After supper we crawled into the tent to try and get a good night's sleep in preparation for climbing Snowdon the next day. We all seemed to sleep well apart from Titch P, who claimed that the ground under the tent was extremely rocky, but nobody else seemed to have had a problem.

The next day (May 7th 1960) dawned cloudy although dry. After breakfast we started off up the Pyg Track before leaving it to climb up towards the summit of Crib Goch, from which the early morning mist was now lifting. We were aware of a large party up ahead of us and when we finally reached the top of Crib Goch (3,023 feet), we saw that it was a group of young army cadets. We took a brief rest and admired the breathtaking views which were unfolding before us. The summit of Snowdon itself was shrouded in cloud, but lesser peaks were clearly visible.

We then set off along the knife-edge Crib Goch

ridge, which we later learnt is one of the four classic ridge traverses in Great Britain. The ridge was very narrow with sharp drops on either side. We were proceeding along the ridge quite steadily when we abruptly caught up with the party of cadets. Much to our amazement they were crawling slowly on all fours along the ridge! There was no way of circumnavigating them as the ridge sides were too precipitous. Unfortunately for them, the only way for to proceed was to clamber over them as carefully as we could without crushing fingers, hands or heads in the process.

The track then rose up to the summit of Crib y Ddysgl (3,493 feet) before dropping down to where the railway track came up from Llanberis. It was then a short walk up to the summit of Snowdon (Yr Wyddfa), at 3,561 feet the highest mountain in England and Wales. We did all feel that the railway and the café on the top of Snowdon were rather an affront to a noble mountain. At least no other mountain in Britain has suffered the same fate. We clambered to the top of the summit cairn before leaving it to the 'day trippers'.

We descended down to the ridge called 'Bwlch y Saethau' (Pass of the Arrows), which figures in Arthurian legend. We then ascended Y Lliwedd before scrambling down to the shore of Llyn Llydaw. From there we walked around the north side of Llyn Teryn and back to our campsite, having completed the Snowdon Horseshoe and had a wonderful introduction to our mountain heritage.

After supper we crawled into our tent and were all soon asleep apart from Titch, who was still complaining about the rocky ground. It was only after the tent was taken down the next morning that the latrine shovel was found embedded in the mud underneath the groundsheet above which poor Titch had been trying to sleep!

We let him sleep in the back of the minibus on the homeward trip back to Northampton. We all agreed that climbing mountains was great fun.

LAKE DISTRICT - THE EXPLORERS

We didn't have to wait too long before being back amongst mountains again. Our 1960s Annual Summer Camp was to be spent in the Lake District. We were going to have our base camp at Stonethwaite Farm in Borrowdale to the south of Derwentwater. Early morning on Monday the 25th July saw our heavily-laden coach leave the school yard on our long journey north.

The major incident of the day occurred on the road between Keswick and Stonethwaite. Our coach was negotiating a tight corner when we were confronted by an army lorry coming at full speed in the opposite direction. It swerved violently, tore through a fence and then ploughed into a thick hedge before coming to rest. Everybody piled out of the coach to see if we could provide any assistance, but fortunately no one was hurt. The lorry itself was well wedged into some small trees, so one of the scouts went to get a felling axe from the coach. However his lumberjacking skills didn't improve one of the lorry's tyres, so it was thought best to go, quickly, and leave the soldiers to it.

We finally reached the campsite at 7.30 pm and started to pitch the tents before darkness came. The camp was in a secluded valley with steeply-wooded slopes and a mountain stream that ran gurgling through the campsite near to the camp kitchen. Water shortage was not going to be a problem – in fact it was too much water later that caused the difficulties!

The Senior Scouts in the troop had been encouraged to submit plans to carry out any climbing expeditions within reason. Chris C, John K, Richard C and myself planned to do our Senior Explorer Badge. We had to cover 80 miles in four days, carrying all our gear with us including food. We also had to complete different projects chosen by each team member. I was to be the expedition's botanist, compiling a list of flora seen. Fifty-two species were noted, many of them being collected and pressed.

We set off on Wednesday the 27th July from the base camp, passing through Seathwaite and climbing up through the Grains Pass down through which flowed the Grains Gill. We were all finding the going rather laborious due to our bulging rucksacks. We had kept the weight as low as possible, even having made the decision to leave the tents' flysheets behind, a decision we were later to regret.

We went over Esk Hause, climbed over the Langdale Pikes and proceeded down to the Wrynose Pass. Heading further south towards Coniston we found a sheltered spot to camp for the night.

The next morning there was a slight drizzle, but it had fortunately stopped by the time we reached the village of Coniston. Our route then took us via Hawkshead and then on to Ambleside at the northern end of Lake Windermere. We soon left civilisation behind us once more as our route climbed up to the head of the Kirkstone Pass in driving rain and low cloud. Visibility was down to about 10 yards but then as we descended down the pass the cloud layer, rather eerily, lifted to a few feet above our heads.

We found a farm to camp at and managed to erect the tents before it began to rain heavily once more with a strong wind buffeting our two frail hike tents. We were now regretting our decision to leave the fly-sheets behind as there was a constant misty spray coming through the tents' walls. When I awoke in the morning I found that I was lying in a one-inch deep inland sea and my sleeping bag was soaked.

It had stopped raining for a while and after breakfast we struck camp. We continued to head down the Kirkstone Pass, past Brothers Water and on towards Ullswater before striking off westwards and starting the long slow climb, in light drizzle now, up towards Striding Edge. This is the knife-edge ridge which leads up to Helvellyn and, like Crib Goch, it is one of the four classic ridge traverses in the British Isles. Climbing along a narrow ridge carrying a heavy rucksack and wearing a cycle cape which acted like a sail was most unpleasant, but eventually, and to considerable relief, we reached the broad summit of Helvellyn (3,118 feet).

That night we camped in a pine forest overlooking Thirlmere. I managed to have an accident with my toothbrush! Whilst planning for our Explorer Hike I had tried to lighten my kit as much as possible. One idea was to make my metal cutlery lighter by drilling holes in the handles. I had then become carried away and drilled some holes in my toothbrush handle too. This was fine for a few days but then the head snapped off in my mouth and I nearly choked on it! I decided not to patent the idea.

The weather improved during the night and the

next morning we walked around the southern end of Thirlmere, over the Wythburn Fells and then descending down into Borrowdale, reaching the base camp by midday. Mission completed! We just then had to write up all our reports and try to get our bedding and clothes dry.

BASE CAMP

On return to Base Camp, our first task was to get dry and dry out our sleeping bags. We noticed that ours were not the only sodden sleeping bags steaming in the sunshine. After our trip to climb Snowdon a few months earlier the new 'yurt' mountain tent had been modified as it had been found to be rather impractical having to crawl through the entrance 'sleeve'. A new doorway had been created in the side of the tent to improve access, which could then be closed with lacing. However Base Camp had also experienced the heavy rain, much as we had in the Kirkstone Pass. Unfortunately the new door had leaked like a sieve and because of the sewn-in groundsheet the tent's occupants were flooded out. At least we could all commiserate together.

We also noticed that the latrines had been moved. These consisted of two square tent-like cubicles which contained the dreaded Elsan chemical toilets. Their original siting had been on a slight slope, with the result that one of the Elsans had toppled over whilst some poor lad was occupying it! A flat hollow area had since been selected.

In the Senior Scouts' camp kitchen area it was decided to build a camp oven. A large square metal biscuit tin was placed on its side upon two lines of stones so that a fire could be lit underneath. Stones were then placed covering the sides and top of the tin and a chimney constructed at the rear. A fire was lit underneath the oven and once the heat had built up the joint of meat (hopefully to be our dinner) was placed inside the oven in a cooking tray. The tin's lid was then pushed back firmly into place to act as the oven's door.

A trip down to the nearest village store was necessary to replenish supplies and Richard S volunteered to stay behind and keep the fire stoked up. The shopping party eventually returned and trooped along to the camp kitchen to see how the dinner was cooking. We immediately noticed that 'le chef' Richard was looking 'different'. He appeared to be rather red in the face, and then we realised that his eyebrows were missing!

The poor lad had apparently removed the lid from the front of the oven in order to see how the joint was cooking, at which point fat from the meat had ignited with the inrush of air with a large flash. At this point we realised that there should have been some venting holes placed in the back of the tin oven. Fortunately Richard remained remarkably cheerful, especially when he was awarded with second helpings and given the evening off from all other duties.

One of the most tedious of camp tasks was the cleaning of the pots, pans and plates after a meal. Hot water in a suitable volume was always difficult to produce, with the fire tending to be dying out at this stage. Then someone had the novel idea to wash everything by using 'hydro-power'. The theory was to utilise the power of the fast-flowing stream which was only a few feet away. All the plates and pots and pans were wedged under water between rocks at the edge of the stream. They were then left overnight for the power of nature to work. Unfortunately further rain fell overnight and by the morning the stream was a raging torrent. There were no plates to be seen – only a few dented pans! Most of the plates and pots were recovered over the next few days, but the exercise was not repeated.

SCAFELL HIKE

After a couple of days at Base Camp spent drying out, it was time to do some more mountaineering. On our

Explorer Hike we had seen Scafell Pike in the distance, and as this is the highest peak in England it was chosen to be our next target. This time the team consisted of John K, Rodney W and myself. Rodney had brought along his father's old hike tent which he assured us was a three-man one which sounded ideal for our climb. Also it was highly waterproof!

As the distance involved was not too far we decided to set off from base camp on the afternoon of Monday the 1st of August. We planned to set up camp in the early evening on Esk Hause and then to climb Scafell Pike, returning to our tent before night fall.

We retraced our previous route from Stonethwaite up to Seathwaite. It was a very hot day and we were grateful to be travelling with relatively light rucksacks compared to the earlier hike. The rain of the previous few days however had made the ground very boggy and it was quite a struggle to squelch up to Esk Hause, which we reached by 6 pm. A secluded spot was found to pitch Rodney's tent and we had supper before heading off to ascend Scafell Pike (3,210 feet). We reached the summit just as the sun was beginning to set in the west, illuminating Wastwater and in the far distance the sea.

It was dusk by the time we returned to the tent, and we were looking forward to getting a good night's sleep. It was then that we realised we had a problem.

Rodney had claimed that his (father's) tent was a three-man one, so John K and I decided that they must have been extremely small men! There was no way there was room for our three sleeping bags side by side. The only way we could fit into the tent was if we all lay on our sides, rather like a plate-rack!

The ground was quite hard and uneven so that periodic rolling over onto the other hip became desirable, but this proved to be difficult unless everyone rolled over in unison. It proved to be a long and uncomfortable night!

Once the sun came up we struck the tent and were on our way. It was quite a relief to stretch our legs as we made our way down the Sty Head Pass. We made good progress in the sunshine and the memories of our uncomfortable night soon faded. The Sty Head Pass joined the Grain Pass at the Stockley Bridge and we were soon passing through Seathwaite en route to Stonethwaite and Base Camp.

The rest of our stay in the Lake District was more relaxing, the weather improved and even my plate turned up after its downstream adventure!

During the long return coach journey to Northampton there was plenty of time to reflect on the highlights of our Lake District adventures. The most memorable event to me was our evening climb of Scafell Pike, which I felt epitomised mountaineering.

This contrasted markedly with our ascent of Snowdon a few months earlier when we had had to share the summit with all the day trippers who had come up on the train. Scafell Pike, even as the highest mountain in England, had not been spoilt by a café or a railway track. It remained an unspoilt natural peak.

It was also greatly enhanced by the fact that we were the only people on the mountain that evening. Even as young mountaineers we had already learnt that you didn't 'conquer' a mountain, you were merely privileged to visit its summit and needed to respect it. After all, mountains have been there for a very long time!

CHAPTER TWO

1961
A WALK IN THE BLACK FOREST

A month after our return from the Lake District, planning was started for our next expedition. It was to be just for the Senior Scout Troop this time. Most of us were due to do our A-level exams during the next summer, so it would take place during the holidays afterwards. It was decided that the expedition would last for 17 days. The first week was to be spent hiking through the Black Forest (Schwarzwald) in Germany

(West Germany as it was then). We were then going into Switzerland for a few days before travelling on to the Allgauer Alps in Bavaria in order to climb some mountains.

It was therefore on the 24th July, 1961, that twelve Senior Scouts and their long suffering scoutmaster set off for Germany. We travelled by train from Northampton to Euston Station, London, and then on the Underground down to Victoria, where we caught a train to Dover and embarked on a Channel ferry (the Königin Elizabeth) to go across to Ostend. There we passed through Customs and located our train for the next leg of our journey.

The train left Ostend at 9.30 pm and we all tried, generally unsuccessfully, to get some sleep, but in reality the journey was far too interesting to miss any of it. We passed through Brussels, Liege and at 1.45 am crossed the German border. We stopped for half an hour at Bad Aachen when the Customs Officers came on board the train.

We passed Cologne and an hour later stopped briefly at Koblenz. After passing Mainz we enjoyed some great views of the River Rhine in the half light of dawn. There were several brooding castles on the hillsides and a number of ships and barges travelling along the great river. The train passed through Worms and then had a stop at Mannheim. Karlsruhe was reached at 7.30 am, where we had to change trains before finally reaching Freiburg, the gateway to the Black Forest. It was now 10am on a fine sunny morning. It had been quite a journey, but we were now looking forward to using our legs again. They were certainly well used over the next five days as we hiked south through the Black Forest, covering over 60 miles on the way down to Tiengen.

En route we walked over Feldberg, which at 4,919 feet was the highest point in the Black Forest. The summit of Feldberg itself was a little disappointing as it was merely the highest point on a raised plateau. Also it sported a café, shades of Snowdon! We descended very quickly under the weight of our rucksacks. Too quickly for Chad W, who went into an uncontrolled series of forward rolls down the steep hillside. Unfortunately each revolution was accompanied by the frying pan, which was tied to the top of his rucksack, swinging over and giving him a clout on the back of his head!

At Tiengen we caught a train to Schaffhausen, in Switzerland, where we camped for a couple of days on the bank of the Rhine, quite close to the famous Rhine Falls. Traditionally scouts always wander off and relieve themselves before finally turning in at night-time when camping, otherwise it's always a nuisance trying to extricate oneself from a sleeping bag in the dark and then once outside there are always guy ropes to fall over. So on the first night, by the Rhine, several of us strolled down the nearby road towards what appeared to be a small power station. Just before reaching it we passed a large field and in the gathering gloom we walked a discreet distance into the field and duly relieved ourselves.

The result was alarming. As soon as the liquid hit the ground there were loud hissing noises, accompanied by clouds of steam. There was also a smell of burning rubber and we all realized that our feet were getting hot! We raced back to the road and tried to work out what had happened. We then realized that the field was in fact covered in hot ash, which must have been removed from the nearby power station. We 'hot-footed' it back to the camp to warn the others!

We then travelled on to Konstanz, where we boarded a steamer to cross Lake Constance (Der Bodensee) to Lindau in Germany. We were unable to find anywhere to camp near Lindau, so we crossed the border and camped that night in Austria.

The next morning we retraced our steps back to Lindau, where we caught a train to Immenstadt, changing there for another train which would take us to our final destination at Sonthofen in the Allgauer Alps, Bavaria.

BAVARIA - THE ALLGAUER ALPS

At Sonthofen we were met by two lads from the local Scout Troop who had very kindly organised a campsite for us which was to be our base for the next week. This was sited about 2 miles from Sonthofen on an island which was part of a drainage system constructed by the Nazis in 1933. The bridge over the river to the island displayed a plaque which apparently stated that it had been built by the Hitler Youth. Still seemed to be pretty sound though!

We spent a couple of days settling in and stocking up with supplies from the nearby village of Altstadten. One of the local scout leaders, Paul S, and a friend of his, Heinz, were going to lead a group of seven of us up some of the nearby mountains. We were due to meet up with them the following morning, Friday the 4th August, and so we turned in early at 9 pm.

The camp was woken up at 1 am by Chad yelling. It seemed that he had been bitten on the foot by an animal which had also ripped the tent door open and removed a foot square chunk out of the tent wall. Richard S had been bitten on the neck. We all rushed out of our tents and chased several shadowy shapes away. We kept watch for a couple of hours, but as nothing else was seen everyone went back into their tents as it was very cold. Later however Richard C got bitten on his arm and I had my arm scratched through the tent wall.

We all got up at 6 am and breakfasted, and those that had been attacked went along to the local small hospital (Krankenhaus), where after waiting for an hour we just had our wounds daubed with iodine by the nuns (obviously not concerned about potential rabies!).

Later that morning the climbing team met up with Paul and Heinz, who had organised some cars to take us up to a village in the foothills. From there we started to climb very steeply for about three hours until we reached the Ob Hut, where we were going to spend the night. We deposited our kit there and after a brief rest we set off to climb the nearby Rotspitze.

There followed a hair-raising ascent during which we had to climb up the bed of a stream and then traverse through a waterfall literally clinging on by our fingernails. When we reached the Rotspitze summit (6,600 feet) we saw a golden eagle circling majestically overhead. There was also a crucifix and a tin box containing a visitor's book which we all duly signed. If the ascent had been hair-raising then we had little hair left following the descent, as we tried to keep up with Paul as he leapt down the side of the Rotspitze like a mountain goat.

We eventually returned safely to the Ob Hut

(situated at 5,300 feet) which we were then able to investigate more thoroughly. We were the only inhabitants that night fortunately. It appeared to be a herder's hut, and one half was a cow shed, fortunately empty that night but which emitted a strong aroma. The other half contained a seven-foot square straw bed. There were also a couple of plank benches and an ancient iron stove.

We started to cook supper on the stove, which then unfortunately fell apart in a cloud of steam, so the meal finally had to be cooked on a wood fire outside. There was no lighting in the hut so we had no choice but to turn in early when it started to get dark. As there was only the one 'bed', we drew straws as to who was going to sleep on it, while the others slept on the floor. However even the 'lucky' five had to sleep on their sides in their sleeping bags as there was so little room (memories of Scafell Pike the year before!)

After a while all went quiet as people gradually dozed off. Then the rustling noises started. Eventually they were located as coming from the depths of the straw bed. We optimistically assumed that some 'small' mice were responsible (and not snakes) and so the bed's occupants all bounced up and down! After this everything seemed to go quiet again and everyone drifted off to sleep.

At about 1 am we all woke up abruptly to the sound

of someone being violently sick. Unfortunately nobody had brought a torch as we had all travelled light (or maybe no-light!). Paul tried to find a box of matches in the dark. Meanwhile by the process of elimination we had deduced that the vomiting noises were being emitted by Mick S. Paul had managed to light some straw and we were able to attend to Mick, although the bed then nearly caught fire. Eventually everyone settled down once more and even the 'mice' were quiet now. They had probably run away!

Even then, Paul and Heinz woke us up at 4 am and cajoled us into getting up for breakfast, which was cooking outside. We then washed, very briefly, in the drinking trough outside and bade our farewell to the Ob Hut.

We set off in the early morning light to climb the Grossen Daumen, which loomed majestically over the Ob Hut. It took us just over two hours to reach the summit of the Gran Daumen, which at 7,450 feet is the highest peak in the range. At one point we had to climb up hanging onto a wire rope which had been secured into the rock face around a buttress. On the summit it was rather sobering to discover two graves plus headstones.

From the Grossen Daumen we crossed several snowfields, seeing a chamois and several marmosets. There were quite a few different species of Alpine flora which I collected. It was then that I found out that Paul was a university student and that his subject was botany! He was a great help with identifying the specimens.

In the far distance we saw the Zugspitze, the highest mountain in Germany. By midday we had reached the summit of the Nebelhorn (7,228 feet) after a rather stiff climb. This was followed by a tricky descent with several difficult traverses. We eventually descended into Oberstdorf on the cable railway (Seilbahn). From there we travelled by train back to Alstadten and were back in camp by mid-afternoon. That evening the whole Scout Troop from Sonthofen, plus some scouts from Stuttgart, all came over to base camp for a grand camp-fire and singsong. We certainly all slept well that night.

We struck camp on Monday the 7th August and were given a rousing send off at Sonthofen station that evening by Paul, Heinz and the local scouts. We travelled through the night and reached Cologne by 8 am, where we changed trains. Brussels was reached just after midday. We managed to find the Youth Hostel in the Rue Dupont where we were going to spend the night. We had dinner at the hostel before settling down to sleep in one of the many dormitories. Apparently during the night Chad went on one of his infamous nocturnal lavatory-seeking expeditions.

Consequently he apparently got lost and spent half the night trying to find the right dormitory, clad only in his pyjama trousers and climbing boots.

The next day, after breakfast, we left the hostel and returned to the station to resume our homeward journey. By 2 pm we had reached Ostend and disembarked on the same ferry which we had come over on. We were back in Dover by 6.30 pm, reaching Victoria by 9 pm, then on to Euston and eventually reaching Northampton by 11 pm.

Our adventures were over for a while but we had certainly enjoyed a great trip and our mountains were getting higher.

CHAPTER THREE

1962
RETURN TO SNOWDONIA

After the expedition to Germany, the following year was very tense for most of us as the impending A-level examinations dominated our young lives because our future (hopefully) university entrance would depend on the results.

Once more we were going to visit Snowdonia. Our trip was planned for later in July, once the exams had finished. This time, instead of camping, we were going to stay in the relative luxury of the Scout Association's climbing hut at Yr Hafod in the Nant Ffrancon Pass near to Llyn Ogwen. We travelled from Northampton in two cars, the journey was quite straightforward, being on the A5 virtually all the way. The Yr Hafod hut was quite a luxury for us, much more comfortable than camping.

The first couple of days was spent practising abseiling down some slabs and outcrops near to the hut. After some initial apprehension we all became quite proficient at sliding down ropes at ever-increasing speed. Unfortunately increased velocity meant increased friction, which meant increased rope burns in sensitive places.

Fortunately we then had a day on an intensive rock-climbing course with Showell Stiles, who was one of the Scout Association's climbing experts. We met up with Showell at his house in the remote village of Croesor. It was a meandering journey via Capel Curig, the Nantgwynant Pass and Beddgelert to Pont Croesor. The road became narrower and more tortuous until we reached the hamlet of Croesor nestling at the foot of Cnicht.

Showell had documented dozens of rock climbs of differing degrees of difficulty on the nearby slabs and cliffs of Yr Arddu. By the end of the day we had become reasonably proficient in the basics of rock climbing, belays and rope handling.

After a few days of scraping off layers of skin it was generally agreed that we should climb some mountains to stretch our legs. From the Yr Hafod hut we gazed northwards across the Nant Ffrancon Pass to where Pen-Yr-Ole-Wen (the hill of the white light) seemed to be beckoning us.

So it was on the 22nd of July that we made the stiff climb up to the summit of Pen-Yr-Ole-Wen (3,211 feet). To the north-east we had a glorious view of the Carneddau range, comprising of Carnedd Dafydd and its twin brother Carnedd Llewelyn. Looking back over the way we had come beyond the sheer drop of the pass we could clearly see what has been described as 'the grimmest cwm in Wales'. Circling Llyn Idwal stood Tryfan, then the Glyders with the Devil's Kitchen in the centre. Then came the sharp sides of Y Garn and Foel Goch.

After a short rest admiring the views, we set off along a wide ridge that led up to Carnedd Dafydd (3,427 feet) which had impressive cwms on either side. We then continued along the ridge which eventually led us up to the summit of Carnedd Llewelyn (3,485 feet) where we had a well-deserved break for lunch.

On the way down, via Craig Llugwy (3,185 feet), we found some pieces of rather old and corroded metal. Skip said that they were most likely the remnants of a World War II aircraft, possibly a German bomber that had crashed on the way back from a raid on the Liverpool docks to the north. Someone found what appeared to be part of a machine gun and then an even more macabre discovery was made. It looked like an airman's flying boot! It appeared to be empty, so these 'souvenirs' were carried back to the hut. Our route took us back down to the eastern end of Llyn Ogwen and along its northern shore until we finally returned to the Yr Hafod hut. It had been a long day.

ADAM AND EVE

After a good night's sleep we awakened to a bright sunny day. It was the 23rd of July. We were going to tackle Tryfan and the Glyders which we had admired the day before from the other side of the pass.

After breakfast we set off eastwards alongside Llyn Ogwen before striking off right up to what is known as the Heather Terrace. Tryfan is said to be the only mountain in Wales that cannot be ascended without the use of hand-holds. After quite a bit of scrambling we eventually reached the crest. On the summit of Tryfan (3,010 feet) there is no cairn, only the two monoliths of stone that are Adam and Eve. Adam is the sturdier of the two and we all took turns to clamber up onto the top of it. Nobody fancied leaping across to Eve, as to overshoot would have been unfortunate!

We were just quietly enjoying the view when there was a tremendous roar of aero engines and we were able to look down onto two RAF jets that shot past below us as they flew down the Nant Ffrancon Pass towards Anglesey.

We then headed south down the other side of Tryfan and turned towards the Glyders. A stiff climb led to the summit of Glyder Fach (3,262 feet). From there the route leading up to Glyder Fawr (3,279 feet) took us past the amazing pile-up of mountain 'wreckage' which is known as 'Castel y Gwynt' – the Castle of the Winds. But then beyond were more and more strange heaps of great columnar stones, looking like some shattered mountain-top Stonehenge. This was Bristly Ridge.

We noisily clattered down from Glyder Fawr to Llyn Idwal, passing the bottom of the 'Devil's Kitchen' (Twll Du – the Black Hole) and eventually returning to the Yr Hafod hut to enjoy a relaxing evening.

Two consecutive days of mountain climbing had left everyone a little weary, so we then had two days of practising our newly-acquired rock climbing skills on the nearby slabs and outcrops. Our batteries were by then recharged in readiness to revisit Snowdon after a break of two years.

SNOWDON REVISITED

We had hoped to get a good night's sleep in preparation for tackling Snowdon once more. However at daybreak some people were complaining that they had had their sleep disturbed by hearing footsteps. No one admitted to nocturnal wanderings, but someone suggested that it might have been the ghost of a German airman trying to find his lost flying boot which had been brought back to Yr Hafod!

After breakfast we went by car to the Llanberis Pass where we parked by the Gorphwysfa Hotel. Low cloud was enveloping Crib Goch and we were soon trudging upwards in increasingly wet and uncomfortable conditions. We renewed our acquaintance with the summit of Crib Goch, but the visibility was poor and likely to deteriorate further so no time was wasted in pressing on along the ridge and then towards Crib y Ddysgl. We saw no other people en route until we neared the summit of Snowdon, where we mingled with the train passengers who had been transported up from Llanberis.

What with the crowds around the summit cairn plus the continuing poor views we decided to continue around the Horseshoe to Y Lliwedd, where we would have our lunch. By the time we had reached it the cloud had partially lifted and we were able to enjoy the views whilst having our lunch in complete solitude. Afterwards we scrambled down the scree slopes to Llyn Llydaw, trying not to bury our companions in a hail of rocks. Although we had been pleased to revisit Snowdon, everyone agreed that in future it would be better to try and avoid the 'tourist season'.

Upon returning to Yr Hafod we found we had some new companions. A patrol of German scouts had arrived to spend a few days at the hut and to discover the delights of Snowdonia. We were all having to share the large dormitory in the hut and whilst the German lads were settling in the rest of us had a quick discussion. We had to get rid of 'the boot' before questions were asked about its possible origin! We discreetly carried it to a quiet spot on the hillside overlooking the Nant Ffrancon Pass and Pen-yr-Ole-Wen. Here the boot was given a solemn burial.

That night there was a rousing sing-song with our new German friends, after which we all had a good night's sleep. Interestingly no further ghostly footsteps were heard.

Y GARN AND 'AUF WIEDERSEHEN'

Our sojourn at Yr Hafod was coming to an end. The morning of the 28th of July dawned fine, visibility was good and on this, our last full day, it was decided to have a reasonably easy climb in preparation for our journey home.

The last remaining 3,000 footer in the surrounding mountains was Y Garn, so this was to be our final target. From the hut we set off in a north-westerly direction to first ascend Foel Goch (the Red Hill). Then from the summit of Foel Goch we headed south along the 'bracing' mile-long ridge up to the large cairn on the summit of Y Garn (3,104 feet).

The weather was kind to us on our final day and from Y Garn we could gaze around with great satisfaction at all the peaks we had climbed during the past week. We all felt that our mountaineering skills had improved by leaps and bounds during this Snowdonia trip and were all looking forward to further mountain adventures in the future.

When and where these would occur was uncertain, as half of the troop had now left school and were heading off to different universities and colleges. Hopefully when our paths crossed again they would be on a distant mountain summit somewhere.

THE MOUNTAINEERING CLUB?

A couple of months after the Snowdonia trip I was in London at the beginning of a five-year undergraduate course which would hopefully result in me becoming a member of the dental profession. The first week at UCL was 'freshers week' when all the societies and clubs would try to entice the new 'fresh-faced' students to join them.

In the common room of the Faculty of Medical Sciences all the groups had tables manned by their most persuasive members. I visited the Rugby Club first, where I was well received (probably helped by being 6ft 4inches tall) and was enrolled for their first training session in Regent's Park a couple of days later.

I then looking around to see what other clubs and societies were of interest to me when I came to the UCH Mountaineering Club. As I approached the table I was very enthusiastically welcomed by a student who introduced himself as the Club Secretary and asked me if I fancied doing a bit of mountaineering. He said a party from the Club regularly went up to North Wales, where they were able to stay at a cottage owned by one of the other teaching hospitals. He asked me if this was something that I might like to try out.

I said that I had done a bit of mountaineering with my Senior Scout Troop, which seemed to impress him as he then asked me about my climbing experience. I told him enthusiastically about our previous trips to Snowdonia, the Lake District and the Bavarian Alps. I then got a bit carried away by telling him about our recent trip to Snowdonia where we had climbed eleven

3,000-foot peaks and had also been on a rock-climbing course where the level of 'V.Diff' (Very Difficult) had been achieved. I finished by enquiring what ropes and equipment the club owned.

I then noticed that the Club Secretary had become rather quiet and appeared rather ashen-faced. He was staring at me wide-eyed, as if I was a modern age Edward Whymper who might lead him and his companions to their doom! Eventually he stammered that he felt that I was too experienced for them as they only really did hill walking. He did say however that if I ever wanted to use the other hospital's climbing cottage then just to let him know. At least I knew that any further mountaineering adventures were going to be down to me!

CHAPTER FOUR

1963
EASTER HOLIDAY

Towards the end of that first university term in the autumn of 1962, my old friend Rodney W (he of the infamous three-man tent on Scafell Pike) contacted many of the Northampton undergraduates who were returning for the Christmas holiday to help him with a charity collection for Oxfam. The idea was for us to visit as many of the Northampton pubs as we could in one evening whilst doing the collecting, plus the odd lubricant as well to keep us going.

I managed to enlist an old primary school friend, Bill K, who was attending a northern university, to join us. During the evening, whilst chatting to Bill, I discovered that he was quite keen to try a bit of mountaineering and so we agreed to plan a trip to Snowdonia for the next Easter holiday.

Our problems were logistical ones with both transport and accommodation. Fortunately Bill's mother was able to give us a lift as far as Corwen on the A5 as she was then driving down to Fairbourne in Barmouth Bay. We had some bus timetables and managed to catch a bus to continue our journey along the A5, past Capel Curig and then along past Llyn Ogwen to where we alighted at the Idwal Cottage Youth Hostel (apparently the oldest YHA location in Wales). This was quite close to the Yr Hafod hut where I had stayed the previous summer. This was the first time either of us had stayed at a Youth Hostel in Great Britain but the accommodation seemed quite adequate and we enjoyed a reasonable evening meal.

We were planning our route for the next day when all of a sudden the lights went out. Initially we thought that there had been a power cut, but then we realised that it was 10 o'clock, the time that we had been told was "lights out". We hadn't realised that it was quite that literal! Fortunately we had torches with us.

The next morning, the 1st of April, we crossed over

the A5 and set off towards Pen-yr-Ole-Wen, which loomed over us on the other side of the valley. It was only eight months since I had been on this mountain with my old scout troop friends, but my life seemed to have changed dramatically in the meantime. I was now a seasoned undergraduate, two-thirds of the way through my first year. The mountain was reassuringly the same, though it seemed just as steep as it had been the year before!

The weather was fine and we were rewarded with magnificent views before proceeding onto the Carnedds (Dafydd and LLewelyn). After lunch we descended via Craig Llugwy down to Llyn Ogwen, finishing with a pleasant saunter around the lake back to Idwal Cottage.

That evening we were better prepared for the 10 o'clock lights out. The next day, the 2nd of April, was also a re-run of the previous summer with our route commencing with the ascent of Tryfan, followed by climbing over the Glyders and the Bristly Ridge, then descending to Llyn Idwal past the Devil's Kitchen. It was a good day's climbing and I was feeling somewhat reassured about how much of the route I had remembered. I think Bill was reassured too!

The next day broke with the sun shining and that morning we climbed Y Garn before returning to the

Youth Hostel to pick up our gear and setting off back along the A5 eastwards towards Capel Curig, as we were going to spend the next couple of nights at the Youth Hostel there. It was a six-mile walk to Capel Curig, so we thought it would be helpful to try and hitch a lift. Fortunately quite soon a Land Rover stopped. It belonged to a local surveyor who was quite interested in where we had been climbing. We soon reached our destination at the Capel Curig Youth Hostel, where we settled in for the evening.

The next morning, the 4th of April, was rather cloudy. We walked back through the village and started along the A4086, which after six miles would take us to the Gorphwysfa Hotel and car park from where the Pyg Track started which would lead us up to Snowdon.

We thought we might as well try hitching a lift again so as to conserve our energy for the climbing. A large limousine stopped, much to our surprise, driven by an attractive young woman who enquired where we were going. We explained our destination and as she was going to Caernarvon via the Llanberis Pass she told us to hop in. Bill got into the back and I climbed into the front and off we sped. Sped being the operative word! The long ridge of Moel Siabod flashed by on the left side. Next came the Pen-y-Gwryd Hotel as the car flew into the Llanberis Pass. We overshot the

Gorphwysfa Hotel and car park by half a mile before we could persuade our driver to stop and let us out! Muttering our thanks, we headed back up the pass to the Gorphwysfa to start off along the Pyg Track.

This was the fourth day of climbing and we were feeling pretty fit by now, so the summit of Crib Goch was reached reasonably effortlessly. Traversing the ridge we entered into cloud approaching Crib y Ddysgl, and unfortunately the cloud persisted all the way up to the summit of Snowdon. The railway was not yet functioning so there were few people around the summit which made a pleasant change. We continued around the Horseshoe to Y Lliwedd before descending to Llyn Llydaw and then back to the Gorphwysfa. Unfortunately we failed to hitch a lift on our way back to Capel Curig, so we felt a bit weary by the time we reached the Youth Hostel.

After supper we discussed our four days of climbing and agreed that it had been very enjoyable and had been a good break from our academic studies. Bill felt that it had been a good introduction to the mountains of Snowdonia for him. All good things have to come to an end though, and the next day was spent enduring a long coach journey back to Northampton. Certainly an incentive to learn to drive a car!

SUMMER VACATION

Once the exams were over in that July (1963), most of the students in my year departed from London either to go home or to go away on holiday to relax from the rigours of that first year. I did neither, as I had been approached by one of my old scoutmasters, Skip T, to help out at the troop's annual summer camp. It was going to be held in Wales, on the coast near to Barmouth. He had also enlisted the help of one of my old scouting colleagues, Chris C, who had previously climbed with me in Snowdonia and the Lake District. Chris had just finished his first year at teachers' training college and was also happy to assist.

We travelled to Barmouth by coach and were duly deposited at the farm where we were to camp for the next two weeks. Our campsite was reached via a steep track up a heavily-wooded hillside, which eventually led to a sloping field near to the top of a hill. The track led over a small, clear stream from which we were to draw our drinking water to save having to go all the way down to the farm each day.

I had been appointed the camp quartermaster and my first task in the setting up of the camp was to organise the digging of the latrines. At previous camps chemical Elsan-type toilets had always been used, but apart from the unpleasant aroma they could also be notoriously unstable, especially on a sloping hillside, as previously described earlier at the Lake District summer camp. They also had to be regularly emptied.

After a couple of hours of hard labour two deep trenches had been dug and some hessian screens erected around them. Rolls of 'Bronco' toilet paper were provided in a waterproof tin, also a hurricane lamp and matches for nocturnal visits if needed. There was also a pile of soil plus a trowel for 'covering-up'.

After a few days of 'use' however it was found that the trenches were filling up rather rapidly, so Skip T decreed that less soil should be used and also that the loo paper should be burnt after use. This proved to be quite a difficult feat and apparently at least a couple of scouts tumbled into the trench attempting it!

A few days later the troop was all in camp having lunch. Suddenly someone said "Does white smoke mean a new Pope has been elected?" When asked why, he replied "There's white smoke coming from the latrines!" Sure enough we then all saw the small column of smoke arising from the latrines up on the hillside. The smoke suddenly became thicker and then flames appeared. "The lats are on fire!" went up the cry and everyone went scurrying up the hill with buckets of water. It transpired that an enterprising scout had found that the best way of incinerating the toilet paper was to dowse it with some paraffin from the hurricane lamp and then throw a match on it. Unfortunately he had rather overdone the amount of paraffin!

It wouldn't of course have been a summer camp if we couldn't find something to climb. Although we were within the Snowdonia National Park we were too far south of the 3,000 footer mountains to be able to climb them. However, Cader Idris ('the chair of Idris') was a respectable 2,927 feet and lay just to the south of us, so a mini- expedition was organised. In local folklore Idris was a giant and the top of the mountain was known as 'Penygader', meaning 'top of the chair'.

We managed to get the whole troop to the top. The weather continued to be good and the camp proceeded uneventfully. On the last day the troop set off on a final walk up the hillside behind the campsite, following the course of our stream which ran down past the campsite.

We had only gone about a hundred yards and were negotiating a route up the side of a small waterfall when we suddenly saw it. There, caught between some rocks halfway up the waterfall, was the bloated body of a dead sheep. The worst thing was that we had been drawing off our drinking water a quarter of a mile further downstream. Fortunately no one had apparently suffered any ill-effects but the lesson was truly learnt - never drink from a stream unless at its source!

CHAPTER FIVE

1965

NORTH OF THE BORDER

Unfortunately, 1964 was a fallow year for mountaineering. Academic study had intensified, and not having transport available meant that escaping to the mountains proved impossible. Attempts to maintain fitness were made by playing rugby, although this often seemed to have the opposite effect!

However during the Easter holiday of 1965, whilst back home in Northampton, I met up again with another old friend from the 40th Scout Troop, Mick S, and we decided to organise a climbing trip for the summer holidays. I had recently been given a Black's Good Companion hike tent for my 21st birthday and so we planned to travel up to Scotland by train, camp and climb some mountains. I had a Gaz cooking stove and we both still had our old scout camping gear. We jointly invested in a 100-foot No.4 nylon climbing rope, so we were all prepared.

One day in late July, Mick and I caught the train at Northampton Castle Station and headed north. We reached Glasgow late on the Friday afternoon and had a few hours to kill before proceeding north. Now I was used to Friday nights in Leicester Square and Soho, but none of this prepared us for a Friday night in Glasgow!

We ventured a short way from the station. It was barely nine o'clock, but the number of inebriated bodies falling down everywhere was unbelievable. Inside one public house that we ventured into, a small guy seated at the bar kept leaning backwards until he fell off his tall bar stool, tipping beer all over himself each time. After a number of attempts at reseating him on his stool and replenishing his beer, his friends eventually tired of his repetitive antics. One of them then had a brainwave. He placed the tall stool upside down by the bar and jammed his friend into it, feet first, so he couldn't fall over anymore. Brilliant! Feeling very impressed, we headed back to the station for the final leg of our journey northwards.

Following our exciting evening out in Glasgow, the next day we eventually reached Fort William, situated majestically at the head of Loch Linnhe. Just outside Fort William we found a farm where we were able to camp for the night.

The next day, the 1st of August, we set out to climb Ben Nevis. The weather was indifferent, cloudy with occasional drizzle and 'Big Ben' was not the most spectacular mountain to climb, although the summit cairn at 4,409 feet is not only the highest point on the plateau massif but the highest point in the British Isles. This makes Ben Nevis the best-known 'Munro'. Scotland has a great system of mountain classification; a 'Munro' is a mountain over 3,000 feet, a 'Corbett' is a peak of 2,500–3,000 feet and a 'Graham' is a hill of 2,000–2,500 feet.

Upon returning to our campsite we had a late lunch, packed up the tent and caught a bus at Fort William to take us down the coast to Kinlochleven, which nestles at the head of Loch Leven. Here we found the start of the Old Military Road which would eventually led us south across the moors to Glen Coe.

THE OLD MILITARY ROAD

Mick and I were very much aware of the weight of our rucksacks as we set off from the village of Kinlochleven and proceeded along the Old Military Road as it slowly wound its way up the hillside. 'Road' was a bit of a misnomer, as it was more of a rough gravel track. It was also quite overgrown and there was little evidence of present use, certainly no signs of vehicle tracks.

After half an hour of steady progress uphill we realised that time was getting on and we needed to find somewhere to camp for the night. The problem soon became apparent that there seemed to be no flat areas where the tent, albeit small, could be pitched. There was only the road itself!

We then came to where the road forked suddenly. To the left, it dipped down the hillside, but then climbed back up again after 30 yards or so and rejoined the 'main road'. It seemed that the lower 'siding' was probably the original route but had been 'straightened' by the higher road. We decided that we had no choice but to pitch the tent on this lower loop and just hope that no one came along the road that night! There was no evidence of recent vehicle use but just in case, as a precaution, we rolled a few large boulders into place, blocking both entrances to the lower loop. It was starting to get dark so we cooked supper and then turned in for the night after what had been a very long day.

It was hours later when we were both woken by the sound of an engine. Something was coming along the

Old Military Road from the Glen Coe end. By the sound it was probably a Land Rover or some sort of 4 x 4 vehicle. Would it come down 'our loop' and encounter our tent blocking the road, or would our road block keep it on the higher route?

We anxiously looked out of the tent and saw the vehicle's headlights cutting through the darkness of the hillside above us. We then realised, with great relief, that it was keeping to the higher track and was passing us by unmolested, the noise of the engine gradually dying away into the distance. That was close! Why on earth should anyone want to drive along that road in the middle of the night? Mind you they could have well asked why should anyone want to camp on that road in the middle of the night? Perhaps a case of "You take the High Road and I'll camp on the Low Road"?

Fortunately no more vehicles ventured along the Old Military Road during the rest of the night and we struck camp immediately after breakfast and continued on our way before any more could.

In fact we saw no one else along the whole length of the road and by midday we were descending a series of zig-zags called the 'Devil's Staircase' down to the pass of Glencoe. We joined the road (the A82) at Altnafeadh where we turned westwards to head along Glen Coe. To the south, on the far side of the River

Coe, loomed the impressive ridge of Buachaille Etive
Mor ('the great herdsman of Etive).

GLEN COE

As we trudged westwards down the glen we passed the
peaks known as the Three Sisters on our left, whilst
to the right was the Aonach Eagach ridge. Soon after
the Three Sisters we espied the dark opening of
Ossian's Cave high up on the hillside. Ossian was a
local bard, and tradition says that he was born in the
cave.

When we reached Achnambeithach, a smaller road
forked off to the right. There was a small sign that
proclaimed the presence of a campsite less than a mile
away, so we decided to head for that and check it out.
The campsite occupied a field between the road and
the River Coe. Everyone else on the site appeared to
have arrived there by car and most of the tents seemed
to be of the framed variety.

We picked our way past them right up to the edge
of the River Coe itself. It was quieter here and we
found a good spot on the river bank looking down to
the waters of the river some 10 feet below us. The river
was quite wide here, with a number of small islands
dotted about, and seemed to be flowing along quite
gently. We did in fact debate about wading out to one

of those sandy islands and camping there in splendid isolation. However we decided to review it again the next day as evening was approaching, so we pitched the tent on the top of the river bank. Even this wasn't easy as we found the ground was too rocky to drive the tent pegs in, so we had to resort to tying the guy-ropes around assorted rocks. The tent had external A-poles from which the tent was suspended, and there was a flysheet which fitted over the whole tent.

After we had had supper we noticed that a strong wind was starting to blow down the pass and some dark-looking clouds were beginning to build up. I was in a deep sleep when the storm suddenly broke. There was an almighty clap of thunder and then the rain started. It was incredibly heavy and the wind was howling as the might of the storm was channelled down the Pass of Glencoe. There was a tremendous drumming noise and the whole tent seemed to quiver with the force of the storm. It felt as if our tent was pitched at the foot of the Niagara Falls.

Then an additional noise could be heard above the drumming, like the crack of a rifle. We heard it again and again. The interior space of the tent was getting smaller – and then we realised what the cracking noises were. They were the tent's nylon guy-ropes snapping! The nylon ropes were relatively thin so as to be light, and they passed through small metal D-rings sewn into the edges of the tent walls. The guy-ropes were fraying where they passed through the D-rings and then ultimately snapping under the strain.

Desperate problems called for desperate measures. We switched on our torches and staggered out into the storm. We managed to lash the tent down using the climbing rope and utilising nearby boulders. We crawled back into the tent soaked through, hoping that we had done enough to stop being blown away down the glen. The storm continued to rage outside and there was the occasional noise of shifting boulders, but we seemed to have stabilised the tent.

Over the noise of the storm we could hear car engines being started. Some of our fellow campers were obviously giving up and driving off into the night. Sleep was very fitful, but as the storm slowly abated it became easier to drift off into a deeper sleep.

I opened my eyes to find dawn was breaking. What a dreadful night it had been! But what was that noise? Although the rain had stopped and the wind had died down, there was a loud rushing sound nearby. I peered gingerly outside through the door flap and an amazing sight met my eyes. Within about eight feet of our tent and only just below the top of the bank, the River Coe was in full spate! Whereas yesterday the river had been a number of meandering tributaries with interspersed islands, it was now a raging torrent stretching from one bank to the other. There was no sign of the island we had contemplated camping on! All the surrounding mountains and Rannoch Moor itself must have been draining down into the River Coe.

I then looked around the rest of the campsite. It was now completely empty except for one small orange tent, similar to ours, right down at the far end of the field. All the frame tents had obviously been unable to weather the storm, but at least their owners all had cars in which to escape!

I examined my poor battered tent. The A-poles looked slightly bowed but all the snapped guy-ropes could be knotted together quite easily. The most surprising thing was that the outer flysheet had changed colour! Whereas the tent underneath was the original orange colour, the flysheet had been bleached almost white by the intensity of the storm.

Low cloud and intermittent showers over the next few days discouraged us from any further climbing, plus the fact that we had now run out of dry clothes. It was a great shame that we had to postpone climbing the great peaks of Glen Coe but I resolved to return at a future date to this spectacular and beautiful place. However I also resolved to avoid camping there the next time!

Mick and I caught a bus from Glencoe village to the

railway station at Bridge of Orchy. From there we travelled back to Northampton via Glasgow once more. It had been a memorable week!

A CUNNING PLAN

By the end of October '65 the pressure on us all was building up. Now in our fourth year, we had a large programme of lectures in a wide range of academic subjects which had to be attended. We were also expected to fit in seeing and treating patients for increasingly complex procedures.

Mike B and I decided that we could do with a short break away from it all to recharge our batteries. Where better to escape to but the mountains? Mike had never done any climbing before, whereas I had now climbed a number of peaks in Snowdonia, the Lake District, Bavaria and Scotland. Our cunning plan was to take a few days off from our studies and travel up to North Wales in Mike's old Austin Ten and do a bit of camping and rock climbing.

Dave W was going back home to Llanelli that weekend and kindly suggested that we spent the Friday night at his parents' home and then continue our journey up to Snowdonia the next day. It sounded a good idea at the time and it was only when we eventually returned to London and studied the map more closely that we realised that we had significantly increased the total length of our journey. It was November, the weather was bitterly cold and there was no heater in Mike's old car. We had to keep stopping every half hour to sprint up and down the road for a few minutes to try and get warm and restore some circulation.

We were well received by Dave's parents and given a very welcome hot meal. Afterwards Dave suggested that we strolled down the road to the nearby Red Dragon pub for a few beers to which we readily agreed. It was very busy in the Red Dragon, being a Friday night. When it was nearing closing time a stentorian voice suddenly bellowed out "Stand for the Anthem!"

We struggled to our feet and I muttered to Dave "I'm impressed. I can't remember ever having sung 'God Save the Queen' in an English pub." He immediately hissed back "Don't you dare! It's 'Hen Wlad Fy Nhadau!" (Of course I knew that was 'Land of my Fathers'... not!) This was followed by the club anthem of the Llanelli RFC 'Sosban Fach', the translation of which is strangely 'little saucepan' apparently!

The next morning before we set off, Dave's dad insisted on checking the oil level in the Austin's engine (he must have realised that Mike didn't really know what went on under the bonnet). Apparently the oil didn't even make it to the bottom of the dipstick! Mr W insisted on filling up the engine with oil. Mike looked on anxiously saying "I hope it's going to be all right, it's not used to oil!"

We eventually set off northwards towards Snowdonia. It was at some point in mid-Wales when we were just starting to descend what turned out to be a very steep hill that Mike had a 'brainwave' about how to save some petrol. Just switch off the engine, depress the clutch and coast down all the hills, then at the bottom just start it again and drive up the next hill. This way we should cut our petrol consumption by half. It seemed such a good idea that we were puzzled why no one else seemed to have thought of it! So he switched off the engine, and down we went.

Slowly at first but then gradually faster we went. It was about then that Mike discovered that the brakes didn't seem to be working quite as well as normal. The road now had quite a few bends in it as well, and as he was preoccupied with the steering he couldn't read the road signs that kept flashing by. I eventually managed to decipher one of the blurred images. It said "Steep Hill – engage low gear." Engage low gear? With the engine switched off we didn't have any gears!

We decided that trying to restart the engine and engage a gear might prove terminal for the engine, already suffering from a surfeit of oil. Our problem was then further compounded because we had come around a corner and were now entering a small village at the bottom of the hill. Our horror increased when we saw there was a zebra crossing in the middle of the village and there were people around!

Mike switched on the headlamps and leaned on the horn. I opened my window through which I screamed and waved. We shot through the village and up the hill the other side and eventually came to a stop. Needless to say Mike never tried his fuel economy idea again!

We eventually reached Snowdonia, and as the light was beginning to fade found ourselves near Nantmor, in the Aberglaslyn Pass, just outside the Clough Ellis Estate. There was a flat area on the roadside verge where the car could be parked and there was a small patch of ground amongst the roadside trees that appeared to be a suitable place to pitch the tent. Mike had never been in the Scouts – in fact he'd never been camping before!

I checked around the edge of the small clearing to make sure there were no elm trees, as they can shed their boughs without warning, and it was my tent! The tent was duly pitched and because it was November and the air temperature was rapidly dropping, a mass of dry bracken was collected and piled up between the walls of the tent and the overlying flysheet in order to make the tent as snug as possible. I then started to cook supper on the Gaz stove whilst Mike wandered around looking for something to do.

Our meal was just ready when Mike announced that he'd set the 'dinner table'! Upon investigation I found that he'd placed two tea towels on the (flat) bonnet of the car and then carefully placed all the cutlery and two glasses of water on the towels. Unfortunately, just then there was a strong gust of wind and all the plates and cutlery disappeared into the gathering dusk up the road and hid themselves amongst the leaves. The next fifteen minutes was spent retrieving them by torchlight, by which time the dinner was cold.

PENDRYNDYDRETH

The next morning (November the 7th) dawned cold but bright. Although there was frost on the ground outside, the inside of the tent was quite warm, no doubt helped by the flysheet and the layer of bracken. Mike was keen to climb his first mountain and I decided that Tryfan, at 3,010 feet, would be a good peak to cut his teeth on, so to speak (apt for a dental student!)

The drive up to the Ogwen valley via the Aberglaslyn Pass, Beddgelert and Capel Curig was quite spectacular with all the autumnal colours. We parked opposite the Youth Hostel and set off up the track towards Tryfan. There were very few climbers on the mountain that chilly November morning and the summit was reached uneventfully. Mike was very pleased to have made his first summit and the decision was made to celebrate that evening after dinner down at the local pub.

By the time we had returned to our little campsite (I was relieved to see the tent was still there) a cold wind was starting to blow. Supper was cooked and consumed inside the tent this time and we then set off for the short stroll to the local pub called the Red Dragon (nearly all the Welsh pubs seem to be called the Red Dragon).

I had also promised to phone home (this was years before ET!) I found a telephone box near to the pub but unfortunately there was no functioning light in it. I was going to reverse the charges (in time-honoured student tradition) and managed to get through to the operator, but she needed to know the name and number of the phone box from which I was calling. This proved to be difficult, as although I had a box of matches with me there were a number of panes of glass missing from the phone box which resulted in the match being blown out after a few seconds. I would read a few letters out and then the match would be extinguished. The woman operator was beginning to get a bit tetchy. Not helped when I said "It's a long Welsh name" to which she replied "Well it would be wouldn't it!" I eventually managed to spell it out – "Pendryndydreth".

After my phone call and a few beers and bags of peanuts, we ventured outside to make our way back to the tent. A strong gale was now blowing with leaves and twigs flying all around us. We eventually found the car, but the tent seemed to have disappeared. There appeared to be a tree now where the tent had been. Closer inspection revealed that a large bough had come down from one of the overhanging trees and had landed between the car and the tent itself. Fortunately it hadn't touched the tent, which was unscathed. "At least," I said to Mike as we pulled the bough away, "another branch shouldn't fall down in the same place." He didn't sound very reassured as he muttered "The rest of the bloody tree could fall down on us though!"

We survived the night without any more falling vegetation and the next day we drove back to London, this time via Northampton, which seemed a lot quicker. We both felt our climbing break had done us the world of good and looked forward to our next foray into the mountains.

CHAPTER SIX

1966
FRUSTRATION

Following our somewhat damp climbing trip to Scotland the previous summer Mick and I decided to look further afield for some mountaineering in 1966. We planned to head for the Austrian Alps and had already joined the British Section of the Austrian Alpine Club (the OAV – Osterreicher Alpenverein) so that we would be able to use their high-altitude climbing huts. Camping in mountain regions seemed to be best avoided if at all possible.

Unfortunately our plans came to an abrupt halt at the end of January when I managed to break my right tibia and fibula playing rugby for UCH down in Reading. I was taken to the local hospital, where I was well plastered. Fortunately for me my team-mates, after the match, were able to persuade the coach driver to come to the hospital to pick me up and transport me with the team back to London. There I was deposited at our own hospital, where I remained supine for the next month. My leg was in plaster for five months and when it 'reappeared', the muscles were considerably wasted. I spent the next few months learning how to walk and then run again.

The summer holiday was spent, not in climbing in the Alps, but camping in Jersey convalescing. Compared with the previous summer in Glen Coe at least the weather was dry, but that was the only positive, as there are no mountains in Jersey!

HEADING FOR THE HILLS AGAIN

Our final year studies were very demanding in the autumn term, but it was now December and we felt it would be a good idea to have a few days away in the fresh mountain air of Snowdonia to recharge our batteries before Christmas. It had been over a year since Mike B and I had visited North Wales due to my broken leg having put paid to any summer climbing trips, but I was now restored to full fitness and raring to go.

Eddie P was very keen to accompany us, especially as he had never been anywhere near a mountain before. He also offered to drive us there in his car so he was added to the team! It was decided that December was too late to be camping in Snowdonia but a chance conversation with one of the medical students, Rex B, was very helpful. Rex was now the honorary secretary of the UCH Mountaineering Club. He said there was still the arrangement with St Mary's Hospital's climbing club to use their cottage up in Snowdonia. Rex undertook to make the arrangements for the three of us to use the cottage.

So in early December we set off in Eddie's car, heading for the mountains. The car was an old large black Austin saloon, the sort of car a dealer would describe as 'a runner', but only just! (In fact its previous owner was Dave W's dad!) Generally it went well but occasionally it would fail to start due to an electrical fault which had been traced to a problem with one of the battery connectors. This was remedied, to a degree, by a stout six-inch nail being fixed through the lead battery post. Occasionally this would loosen, resulting in a poor contact and the engine failing to start. But the solution was found by simply giving the nail a sharp tap with a hammer, which Eddie kept under the driving seat just for that purpose.

We reached Snowdonia and in the gathering dusk stopped at a lonely petrol station. A young lad came out and filled up the tank (this was long before self-service pumps). The car then 'decided' not to start, so Eddie lifted up the bonnet and went to get his hammer. I can still remember the look of absolute astonishment on the young lad's face as he watched Eddie smack the battery with his hammer and the engine subsequently roaring into life!

We eventually found the St Mary's climbing cottage near Drws-y-Coed in a narrow valley which ran from Rhyd-Ddu down to Nantlle.

CRIB GOCH

We had a good night's sleep and the following morning set off to drive back through Rhyd-Ddu down to Beddgelert, where we took the A498 past Llyn Dinas and Llyn Gwynant up to the junction with the A4086 where we turned left down the Llanberis Pass. We soon approached the Gorphwysfa Hotel on our right and drove into the car park opposite, where we left the car. There was already a light covering of snow over the ground as we set off to climb Crib Goch, the first peak on the Snowdon Horseshoe route which would eventually lead to the Snowdon summit.

One of the major problems taking a novice climbing, especially in the winter months, is that they don't have the most suitable gear. Eddie had borrowed some Spanish fell boots, but the grip on the soles left a lot to be desired. I had taken them into the Prosthetics laboratory and cut a number of grooves into the soles using an abrasive disc. Eddie had also borrowed a hat, gloves and by the look of the fit, an anorak. I was the only one to own a rucksack so spare sweaters, food and a large bottle of water were packed into it, plus a large plastic bivouac sheet. I was also the only one to possess an ice axe. We also had my 100-foot nylon climbing rope (I had bought out Mick S's share) which Mike and Eddie took it in turns to carry.

From the start of our climb up the steep track the visibility was down to about 100 yards and this became worse as it started to snow gently. We only encountered one other group of climbers, who passed us halfway up Crib Goch and soon disappeared into the mist. I felt that our progress was rather too slow for my liking, not helped by the fact that I was the only one who knew what a long way we had to go that day.

After what seemed hours we finally reached the summit of Crib Goch and the other two sat down expecting a good rest. However I was anxiously scanning along the Crib Goch knife-edge ridge along which we now had to traverse, so I goaded them back into action. The wind speed had now increased and snow and ice particles were blasting up both sides of the ridge to bombard us as we slowly started along the knife-edge. After fifty yards our eyelids were becoming frozen open, except for Eddie whose, eyelids were freezing in the closed position!

Eventually we had traversed the most exposed section of the ridge, but now our progress was getting slower and slower. This was not helped by Eddie repeatedly impeding himself whilst carrying the rope. He kept letting the rope become uncoiled which then wrapped around his legs causing him to fall to his knees. Whilst down on his knees he seemed to be praying. I wasn't sure what he was praying for, but it didn't seem to help in speeding up our progress. The temperature was now falling noticeably, not surprising as we were on an exposed 3,000-foot high ridge.

The snow was coming down more heavily and the light was beginning to fade although it was only three o'clock. I realised that reaching the summit of Snowdon was out of the question now, but I hoped that if we could get over the next summit of Crib-y-Ddysgl and then reach the Snowdon Mountain Railway track we would have a safe escape route down to Llanberis (the train does not run in the winter). However the route was now icing up badly and we all started to slip over, not helped by the fact that we only had one ice-axe between us and no crampons. I felt that our only choice was to bivouac here on the ridge for the night, to which my comrades reluctantly agreed.

Having made our decision to bivouac we had to find the best available spot. Ideally we needed to dig a deep hole in the snow, but the ridge on which we were marooned was quite exposed and the deepest snowdrift we could find was only a couple of feet deep in the lee of the ridge. Using the ice-axe and our hands we dug the deepest hole possible, lined the hole with the bivouac sheet, all sat down in the hole and pulled the sheet over our heads as the roof. We loosened our bootlaces to try and maintain a good blood circulation to our feet. The time was now 4 pm and it was quite dark.

We ate some semi-frozen chocolate and each had a sip of water. The water was already quite cold and in an attempt to try and stop it freezing I placed the plastic water bottle between my legs. We realised that it was important to keep awake, otherwise hypothermia was likely to set in and ultimately 'permanent sleep!' We agreed to undertake 10 minute 'wakey-wakey' calls and to take it in turns to keep talking. It was going to be a long night! We shared life histories, likes, dislikes, our teachers and colleagues. Religion, science, schooldays, girl-friends, food, career aspirations, all were discussed.

The air temperature seemed to be dropping and peeping out from under the bivvy sheet we could see that it had stopped snowing and the wind had dropped. The night sky was alight with thousands of stars, which seemed so close as to be almost touchable. We realised that our body core temperatures were dropping, which was confirmed when I discovered that the water bottle was now frozen! We were just about managing to keep awake, although we had to increase our intermittent shouting and shaking of each other.

I began to worry about my two companions who had put their trust in me to safely lead them over the mountains. I began to think of the nightmare scenario of having to break the news to their families that they had perished on Snowdon. Edward Whymper's famous words kept coming into my thoughts; "Climb if you will, but remember that courage and strength are nought without prudence, and that a momentary negligence may destroy the happiness of a lifetime. Do nothing in haste; look well to each step; and from the beginning think what may be the end."

Fortunately such thoughts dispersed as it started to get lighter, although the snow had started to come down again. By 8 am the visibility had sufficiently improved for us to be able to continue on our way. We managed to slowly stand up and then to start jumping up and down to try and restore our circulation. We staggered on up and over Crib-y-Ddysgl and eventually found the snowed-up mountain railway track, which we followed up to the closed and shuttered Snowdon café. It was only a short way up to the summit cairn itself. It was the fourth of December and my fourth ascent of Snowdon. It was also the only time I ever reached the summit of Snowdon to find that, apart from my two comrades, there was no one else there!

We had a quick photo-shoot and then set off on our descent. We had decided that we would abandon our original plan to complete the Snowdon Horseshoe route. We just wanted to get down as quickly and as safely as possible. We therefore chose to follow the railway track all the way down to the terminus at Llanberis in the bottom of the valley. When we ultimately reached Llanberis a very welcome breakfast was consumed in a little café. Afterwards we managed to hire a taxi to take us back up the Llanberis Pass to be reunited with Eddie's car, which was standing very forlorn and encased in snow in the car park.

A couple of days later we were back at the Dental Hospital. We were fortunate in only suffering from some localised first degree frostbite to a few finger tips as a result of our 16 hours in a snow-hole. Our notoriety amongst our colleagues was considerably increased by our latest exploit. We even formed our own inclusive 'Snowdon Survivors society' with our own special tie!

CHAPTER SEVEN

1967

ESCAPE TO THE HILLS

The Spring Term of 1967 was proving especially arduous. The ultimate part of our Finals examinations was due in the Summer Term, so clinical quotas had to be completed and all the revision lectures and tutorials attended. I didn't even have the diversion of playing rugby, as I had prudently decided that it would be unwise to risk playing again before I qualified, as no more time could be lost to injury. I did try refereeing a few games, not particularly successfully as, like many rugby players, there were a few laws I was a little unsure about!

We three 'Snowdon Survivors' therefore decided that we needed a few days away from the academic pressure to recharge our batteries, thus allowing us to peak for the finals. Another of the lads in our year, Julian B, had expressed an interest in accompanying us on our next trip, especially as the weather was becoming milder. We planned to take a few days off at the beginning of March and duly spoke to Rex B to ask him to arrange for our stay at the St Mary's climbing cottage again up in North Wales. Mike had also purchased another car and was keen to try it out on a long journey.

So once again we were escaping to the hills. As we crossed the border into Wales the weather deteriorated and the rain fell with increasing intensity. As we approached Snowdonia there were large amounts of surface water on the roads. Going through one village the main street was submerged to a depth of over a foot. We were nearly through the flooded section when the car's engine cut out!

A number of local volunteers kindly helped to push us onto dry ground. Unfortunately the engine failed to restart, but one of the locals suggested leaving it for ten minutes and then trying again as hopefully the electrics should have dried out sufficiently by then. His advice was very helpful and sure enough the engine fired back into life and we were on our way.

It was quite dark by the time we reached the cottage at Drws-y-Coed and it started to rain again as we started to unpack the car. Eddie was stationed inside the cottage with strict instructions just to pile up the gear in the living room and not to do anything with it.

We had nearly unpacked the car when there was a scream from inside the cottage. Upon investigation we discovered that Eddie had somehow managed to hang himself by his finger from a sort of meat-hook that was suspended from the living room ceiling. Contrary to instructions, he had thought he would just hang the ice-axe by its wrist-strap loop from the hook. He apparently couldn't quite reach, so he had jumped up to try and flick the loop onto the hook. Unfortunately the only thing that he managed to place on the hook was his index finger and had suffered a very nasty tear along the length of the finger resulting in a large skin flap! We all agreed that it looked as if some embroidery was necessary and that it would be a good idea if he had a tetanus shot as well.

The nearest village was Nantlle, which was further down the valley, so we all got back into the car and set off, having bandaged up his finger as well as we could. Fortunately we managed to find a doctor's surgery still open and Eddie was duly repaired. We made our weary way back to the cottage to rustle up a meal and finally to try and get some sleep in order to get our strength up for the mountains the next day.

FREE ALES

The next day was dry and sunny. Eddie seemed none the worse after his accident and said that he was quite happy to come and watch us fall off some rock faces. We drove down to Croesor and demonstrated some climbing techniques to Julian on the nearby slabs on Yr Arddu, where Mike had had his initiation over a year before.

Later in the afternoon we drove north back to the cottage. Halfway along the road between Rhyd-Ddu and the cottage we passed an old stone barn on the left-hand side of the road. There on the roadside wall of the barn was daubed in two-foot high letters the slogan 'FREE WALES'. We all felt that this was a bit of an affront to our 'Britishness'. There was always a bit of friendly nationalistic banter between the Welsh and English elements in the hospital rugby club at that time, but that was merely a reflection of the rivalry between our national teams.

When we arrived back at the cottage we consumed a few bottles of Julian's home-made ginger beer which he had kindly brought along. This revived our spirits and a plot was hatched to 'embellish' that slogan after dark later that evening. In one of the cottage's outhouses I found a tin of lilac-pink paint plus some brushes. These were placed in the boot of Mike's car and we headed off back up the road to Rhyd-Ddu, past our later target, to visit the Inn there. After a 'few' beers we felt an 'artistic' urge coming on and so the paint hit squad piled into Mike's car and headed back down the now dark and deserted valley.

Mike parked the car on the opposite side of the road with the headlights illuminating the barn wall. There appeared to be a ramp of soil up against the lower part of the wall and the would-be artists charged forward as if going into battle in a hail of muck and bullets. Fortunately there were none of the latter but plenty of the former, as the perceived ramp of soil proved to be a large heap of manure!

Undeterred the 'artists' quickly got to work. "FREE WALES' became 'FREE ALES' and the separatist logo was changed into a large insect. A few other nationalist slogans of another Celtic nation were then daubed on the wall so that the English would not get blamed (that was the theory!) Unfortunately over-enthusiasm also resulted in one of these slogans also being emblazoned on the road going down the hill. We all then leapt back into the car and continued on our way back to the cottage. A hard day's night!

ENTRAPMENT!

The next morning we drove back up the valley and happened to pass the farmer who looked after the St Mary's cottage. He turned and seemed to give us a rather hostile stare as we went past.

Our destination was the Ogwen Valley, where we were going to teach Julian some mountaineering techniques. We climbed Pen-yr-Ole-Wen and then went on to climb the two Carnedds before completing the circuit via Craig Llugwy and descending to Llyn Ogwen and returning to the car park.

We had returned to the cottage and were just preparing supper when there was a loud knock on the front door. Mike went to the door to be greeted by a policeman who wanted to know the owner of the car parked outside. Mike admitted that it was his and had to go outside where the officer showed him some traces of lilac pink paint on the boot lid. The policeman said that someone had done 'some painting' on a barn down the road using a similar coloured paint. He said that he could get the paint samples all tested but perhaps it would be easier for all concerned if the perpetrators just owned up? He seemed rather surprised that there were four of us involved.

It seemed that the paint we had used actually belonged to the farmer who took care of the cottage. To make matters worse it was also the farmer's own barn that we had decorated!

The next morning it was a rather subdued quartet who climbed Tryfan before setting off back to London. It was difficult to know which we were least looking forward to, our Finals or the outcome of our artistic endeavours!

GUILTY M' LORD!

It was nearly two months later that all four of us received a 'short letter' from Caernarvon stating that each of us 'without lawful authority or excuse, did paint and inscribe certain letters upon the surface of the said highway'. Much to our surprise no mention was made of our redecorating the barn, which we had considered to be our major artistic achievement. There had only been three letters on the said highway!

Eddie was all for contesting the complaint, suggesting we had actually improved the road surface. We managed to persuade him that this course of action was probably unwise and quite likely would result in us being deported to Van Diemen's Land.

We had been invited to appear before the local magistrates in June but had to decline, as this would have been in the middle of Finals. So we all pleaded guilty in writing, paid our fines and then concentrated on our revision.

TROUBLE UP TRYFAN

Following the completion of our Finals in July 67 (and before getting the results) several of us decided to escape from London for a few days to recover from the ordeal. There was Mike, Eddie and myself, plus a new would-be mountaineer from our year, David W. On our last two climbing trips to North Wales we had used the St Mary's cottage, but following the graffiti incident we deemed it prudent to stay somewhere else.

We planned to stay overnight at a bed and breakfast place in Corwen on the A5 on our journey up to Snowdonia. We were then going to climb Tryfan the next day, traverse the Glyders and camp that night near to the top of the Devil's Kitchen. Most of our fellow students thought our climbing trips were best avoided by sane beings, especially after our emergency bivouac on Snowdon the previous winter. However this was now summertime and David W thought it would therefore be quite safe to come along with us. How wrong could he be!

Our journey up to Corwen had been uneventful and we had all enjoyed a good night's sleep. Before leaving

Corwen we managed to buy a bottle of white wine from the local butcher's shop. We proposed to drink it, in true Edward Whymper fashion, at our camp that evening to celebrate the end of Finals. We left the car in the car park at the end of Llyn Ogwen and set off to climb the north-east face of Tryfan in the warm sunshine. We were quite well laden with two tents, gaz stove, food, climbing rope and a carefully packed bottle of wine.

Steady progress was made and we eventually came to the final stretch, which involved a bit of 'scrambling' up some slabs to reach the summit where 'Adam and Eve' awaited. I had climbed up and over the final slab, followed by Eddie, when there was a shout from below. It was Mike who informed us that David was stuck. Peering back down the final face I could see that David was not so much stuck but rather he was clinging to the rock surface, ashen-faced and with his eyes shut.

All entreaties to proceed failed and it was decided that the only way to get him up would be by pulling him up using the rope. I lowered a sufficient length of rope down to Mike, who was standing just below David, for him to secure it around David's waist with a bowline knot. Once he was securely attached, Eddie and I, who were now safely anchored, would then pull him up. That was the theory anyway! The problem was that Mike (not having unfortunately been a Boy Scout) now admitted in a loud voice that he'd forgotten how to tie all the knots that I had been teaching him in preparation for our trip to the Alp a few weeks later!

Apparently the only one he remembered was the granny knot, which is not so much a knot as a reef knot tied incorrectly. Mike said he realised it would probably unravel, but if he tied lots of them they should hold for long enough for us to be able to pull David up before they all came undone!

This revelation did absolutely nothing for David's confidence and he now started to moan gently. However it did work in practice, and we quickly hauled him up and over the edge. He then continued to crawl on all fours over a more or less flat surface, still attached to the rope, to the summit! This was much to the amazement of the crowd of people who were sitting there eating their sandwiches and admiring the view.

David eventually recovered enough to be able to continue in the hope that the worst was now behind him. He was also encouraged by the thought of the wine later. We traversed the Glyders without further incident and with the sun beginning to go down found a sheltered spot to pitch the two tents. A nearby stream issued forth from the mountainside and the bottle of white wine was reverently placed securely between some rocks in the stream to chill.

Having finished supper and with the setting sun

emitting a wonderful orange glow over the distant hills to the west, we carefully uncorked the bottle of wine. We filled our glasses, held them up to the fading sun's rays and toasted to our future success in dentistry. We then let the chilled amber liquid gently flow into our mouths and over our taste buds. That wine which had been so carefully transported up the mountains tasted... absolutely awful! Still, what can you expect if you buy wine from a butcher's shop?

THE AUSTRIAN TYROL

Results day finally dawned when we all had to go down to London University's Senate House in Malet Street. There is probably no easy way to get exam results, and there was already a large crowd of students all anxiously perusing the ranks of notice boards. It was an advantage being tall, and Mike and I were soon able to confirm that our names were indeed on the list. One poor girl was becoming quite hysterical because she couldn't see her name on the list. However she soon felt much better when, from my vantage point, I saw her name higher up on the notice board amongst those who had achieved honours!

After the stress of Finals there was more a feeling of relief than euphoria initially. The general public was to be spared our attentions for a few further weeks until our names were officially entered onto the Dentists' Register.

Mike and I had already decided that we needed to recuperate from the exams irrespective of the results and had planned a couple of weeks climbing in the Austrian Tyrol. We were now both members of the Austrian Alpine Club and had arranged our travel via them. We both had equipped ourselves with crampons and Mike had also purchased an ice axe. I had also given him more instructions in tying knots, although I still had some doubts about his ability.

We duly met up at Victoria Station at the end of July and set off for the continent. The Channel crossing was quite smooth and we continued the journey on the overnight sleeper train to Austria. The word 'sleeper' seemed to be something of a misnomer – I don't think I slept a wink.

When we reached Tyrol we continued our journey by bus up to the small village of Obergurgl in the Otztal Alps. At 6,330 feet, Obergurgl is the highest parish in all of Austria. We found a small guest-house on the outskirt of the village, and the lady who owned it recommended a local restaurant where we enjoyed a very pleasant dinner of Wiener schnitzel and a few beers. A pleasant euphoric feeling settled over us as the realisation finally settled in that after five long years, we were undergraduates no more!

Following a good night's sleep and a hearty breakfast we set off the next morning up the valley, rucksacks on our backs and a spring in our steps. Alpine flowers adorned the ground either side of the path, the mountain air felt crisp and intoxicating, and all around the snow-capped peaks and glaciers appeared to beckon us on.

By midday we had reached the Schonweiss Ski Hut. There was a large veranda on the south side of the hut, very popular with other walkers and which offered a wonderful vista of the surrounding peaks. We sat there enjoying the view and a couple of beers and decided that the Schonweiss would make a good base for a couple of days. What a peaceful, relaxing spot.

All of a sudden there was a crashing sound from the other side of the narrow valley. A number of rocks could be seen bouncing down the mountainside and landing on the track which ran along the valley floor. We found this a bit alarming, especially when it happened again during the afternoon at different sites. This didn't happen in Snowdonia!

We realised that by midday the sun was softening and melting ice higher up the mountain slopes, which was then releasing stones and rocks. These were then rolling down the mountainside, seeking unsuspecting heads to land on. This was the reason why Alpine climbers rise early, before dawn, and so can be well

1967 – JF at the top of Hangerer

JF on Hangerer

1967 – JF on Festkogel

JF relaxing on Festkogel

1970 JF and Mike on Ruderhof Spitze

1970 – JF on Glyders

JF on the Wildspitze

1970 - Mike and JF ascending the Wildspitze

1970 - JF on Snowdon

Three men up a mountain (Snowdon)

back down the mountain before midday when the rocks and roll starts! Early nights and early starts seemed to be advisable.

We approached the lady innkeeper of the Schonweiss to enquire if there was any available accommodation. She did have one room available which she showed to us. It was quite basic and instead of beds there was a large raised 'sleeping platform' (Matratzenlager) on which to place one's bedding. We had sleeping bags with us so gratefully accepted and went down to the dining room to have our evening meal.

Neither Mike nor I had studied German at school, both having 'learnt' French and Latin. The menu was all in German, so to play safe we stuck with Wiener schnitzel again. We couldn't decipher the desserts part of the menu, but we noticed that a couple at the adjacent table appeared to be enjoying an attractive looking 'pudding'. We managed to enquire what their dish was called and they said "Kaiserschmarrn". We called over the waitress and managed to persuade her that we would now like to have some 'Kaiserschmarrn'. She seemed rather surprised at our request but eventually reappeared with two very large bowls of what turned out to be giant chopped-up pancakes amply filled with fruit. It took us about half an hour to devour this repast and we both felt completely stuffed and rather sick.

Later on in our holiday we discovered that 'Kaiserschmarrn' was normally regarded as a main course. Also that the literal translation apparently is 'Emperor's rubbish'. We certainly slept well after it!

HANGERER

We slept well after our enormous supper and couldn't face any breakfast the following morning, the 1st of August. The peak of Hangerer loomed large over the Schonweiss Hut, but en route we first climbed the nearby Halsl peak at 8,560 feet. Although still early morning the mountain air was already warm and we were sweating quite profusely by the time we reached the summit of Hangerer at 9,950 feet.

Having witnessed the rock falls the previous afternoon we didn't dwell for too long on the summit before starting our descent. On the way down we encountered a steep snow slope. I thought this would be an ideal spot to try glissading. A few months previously, in an attempt to relax from my academic studies, I had browsed through Gaston Rebuffat's excellent book entitled 'On Snow and Rock'. In this he described the technique of glissading as a method of descending on hard snow which had softened on the surface. Basically it is a controlled slide, with the body in a crouched position, knees bent and using pressure on the ice-axe for the purpose of braking.

Mike looked on rather dubiously as I set off down the slope, which quickly proved to be somewhat steeper than it had first appeared. My speed built up alarmingly and downward pressure on my ice axe didn't appear to be having any braking effect. I then leant back too far, which resulted in me sitting down and tobogganing down the slope on my backside at an increasing speed. It was probably fortunate that the snow then petered out into a rocky scree slope which had a braking effect, albeit somewhat uncomfortably on my posterior, and I ground to a halt.

Mike carefully walked down the snow slope and enquired about my health. Feeling was gradually being restored, fortunately the cold of the snow had quite an anaesthetising effect. A new treatment for haemorrhoids perhaps?

The rest of the descent was uneventful and an hour or so later we were once more sitting on the veranda outside the Schonweiss enjoying a beer.

THE VALKYRIES

We were just contemplating having another beer when the lady innkeeper of the Schonweiss approached us and asked if we would mind three German girls sharing our Matratzenlager with us that night. Trying not to sound too enthusiastic, we said that would be fine with us. We then had another beer to celebrate our good fortune.

However our euphoria later evaporated when we espied the three girls in the dining room at supper time. To say that they were large would have been an understatement. We became increasingly surprised at the large amount of beer they were consuming. What was even more unsettling was the sidelong glances being made in our direction, which were accompanied by much giggling.

In the end we thought a discreet withdrawal from the dining room was the best move and crept off to our Matratzenlager. Here we faced a dilemma. Instead of beds there was just the raised sleeping platform which we had had to ourselves the previous night, but tonight the three mighty maidens would be sharing it with us! The most desirable space was adjacent to the wall, and we decided to draw cards to determine who was to be the lucky one. Mike lost – I was surprised that he had agreed to use my pack of cards. We wanted to be away early in the morning and climbed into our sleeping bags fully clothed. We pretended to be asleep when the three maidens eventually came up to the darkened room. There then followed a series of zipping noises and poppers popping, accompanied by much giggling which went on for several minutes. Eventually all went quiet and I nodded off to sleep.

The room was just starting to get light the next morning when Mike shook me awake, whispering "It's time to go". There was a chorus of very loud snoring noises coming from nearby. We quietly packed our sleeping bags into our rucksacks and it was then that I noticed that Mike had built a veritable Maginot Line of crampons and ice-axes between himself and the Valkyries!

We went downstairs, paid our bill and quietly left the Schonweiss.

A ROLLING STONE...

An hour or so after leaving the Schonweiss we were descending a zig-zagging track down a steep hillside towards Obergurgl. Mike stumbled and accidentally dislodged quite a large boulder that went careering off down the hillside. It was only then that we noticed two figures sitting about 100 yards or so below us, with their backs towards us as they sat admiring the view. Initially it appeared that the boulder would pass well to the left of them, but then it gave an enormous bounce and veered right, aiming straight at them like something out of an Indiana Jones movie. We both started to yell in an attempt to get their attention to their impending doom. "Below!" (the mountaineer's equivalent of "fore"), "Achtung!" and "Ausfahrt!" (??)

After what seemed like an eternity the couple finally turned around and looked up the hillside, by which time the boulder only seemed to be 10 feet above them. It then hit a small outcrop and split into two, with the two pieces passing them harmlessly on either side. As we gazed down with great relief, the couple looked up the hillside towards us and, much to our amazement, gave us a friendly wave to show that they were all right!

We continued our descent, very slowly and carefully now, eventually reaching the spot where the pair were still sitting. They turned out to be a very pleasant middle-aged Austrian couple who were profuse with their thanks to us for having alerted them to the imminent danger. They seemed quite oblivious to the fact that we had created the danger in the first place!

To make matters more embarrassing for us, we kept meeting up with the couple around Obergurgl over the following few days. At each encounter they seemed to be describing us to everyone as their saviours! It was one of the few occasions when our lack of ability in speaking German actually helped us!

We eventually got back down to the village, thankfully without further incident. We returned to the guest house where we had stayed before and fortunately managed to book in there again. We then spent a couple of relaxing days exploring Obergurgl and planning our next target, which was to be the Zirmkogel, the highest peak locally.

DONNER UND BLITZEN!

A few dark clouds were scudding across the early morning sky on the 4th of August as we left Obergurgl along a steep track which we had reconnoitred the day before. The path went up through a pine forest which gradually opened out into Alpine pastures. There was the sound of cow bells in the distance, probably as the cattle were descending into the valley for the morning milking, but we saw no herders. In fact we saw no people for the whole of the day. We had either chosen a remote or difficult peak to climb or word had got round that it was safer to avoid the two English climbers!

As we toiled up a broken ridge which would lead us to the top of the Zirmkogel, the sky grew ominously darker with approaching storm clouds. The atmosphere became more stifling and uncomfortably warm. We had just reached the summit of the Zirmkogel at 10,610 feet when the sound of thunder began to rumble around the surrounding peaks and it became darker still. We decided that this was no place to hang around and quickly started to retrace our steps back down the mountain.

After a few minutes we both noticed a peculiar clicking noise that sounded very much like a Geiger counter. The clicking became louder, as did the rumbles of thunder. The noise seemed to be behind me – in fact whichever way I turned it was behind me! I then discovered that it was coming from the uncovered metal spike on the end of my ice-axe. This was strapped to the back of my rucksack with the steel point projecting upwards about a foot above my head! Static charge seemed to be building up in the spike. Could it be the precursor to a lightning strike?

I quickly removed my rucksack, dropped it to the ground and we dived for cover behind some nearby rocks.

After a few minutes nothing appeared to be happening except that the clicking noise had now stopped and a heavy downpour of quite cold rain had started. A couple of minutes later we decided that we needed to get down off the mountain as quickly as possible. I put my rucksack back on and we raced off down the broken ridge that we had so laboriously ascended half an hour before. However, each time we had to climb over an outcrop on our descent my ice-axe started to click once more. I noticed that Mike was dropping further back behind me, and at the same time stones and rocks were starting to bounce down adjacent gullies. I called back to him to close up, to which he shouted back "I'm not coming anywhere near you!"

We made it down safely, but after that we contrived to carry our ice-axes in a different way so that they less resembled lightning conductors! This involved clipping a karabiner onto the top ring of one of the two rucksack carrying straps and then just threading the spike and haft of the axe through it so it rested between back and rucksack. Sounds uncomfortable, but it didn't prove so.

Back in the Obergurgl guesthouse we enquired where we could dry out any clothes. We were pointed in the direction of a clothes line in the garden and thought this would be a good opportunity to wash any clothes too and then hang them all out together. Unfortunately it rained hard that night and the next day as well, so we were trapped in Obergurgl because our only remaining dry clothes were the ones we were wearing!

It wasn't until the 7th of August that we felt we could safely go forth once more. Our final target was to be the Festkogel at 9,996 feet, and we fairly raced up the mountain, utilizing all the energy we had been storing up over the past few days. The sun shone and the views were magnificent. On the descent we went past the ski station terminus on the ski lift, which only worked in the winter months. We realised that during the summer months Obergurgl was enjoying its quiet season and apparently really came to life in the winter time as Austria's highest ski resort. Mike and I had never been skiing, but this would certainly be a good place to come and learn.

Our return journey back to England was uneventful and we both felt restored and invigorated by our Alpine trip and were now ready to start work.

SILENT NIGHT

Back in London once more, the mountaineers were all having to get used to the reality of working for our living. Our student days were now over and we were having to put into practice all the things we had been learning about, studying and practising for the last five years.

Mike and Eddie were going into general practice. I was staying at UCH doing a general duties house surgeon job and Julian was at UCH too as a resident house officer (RHO). One of the advantages of the RHO job was that accommodation was provided in the hospital. The downside was being on call at night time and over the weekends. Most RHOs were quite worn out by the end of their six-month stint and Julian was proving to be no exception.

I offered to cover for him one night to try and ensure that he had at least one good night's sleep to recharge his batteries. A spare room was found for me in the residential block, so I retired early to try and get at least a little sleep before being called. In fact I had rather a lot of sleep and had a completely undisturbed night.

I sauntered down to the refectory for breakfast in the morning feeling rather refreshed. There I was surprised to find Julian looking bleary-eyed and indeed considerably worse than he had been the day before. I enquired if he hadn't been able to get off to sleep. He replied that getting off to sleep hadn't been a problem but that he had been woken up at 2 am by the switchboard to say that they hadn't been able to rouse me on the telephone and therefore could he come down to see the dental emergency that had arrived in the main hospital's casualty department! I hadn't heard the phone at all in my deep slumber.

I felt somewhat embarrassed that my attempt to help Julian had failed so miserably. However I did suggest, in an attempt to make amends, that we should arrange another weekend climbing trip to North Wales at the earliest opportunity. Julian brightened up considerably at the idea and wondered if we could go up Snowdon as he hadn't climbed that peak yet and would like to add it to his list of conquests.

SMELLS FISHY!

It was therefore a few weeks later, on a Saturday morning in late October, that Julian and I set off for North Wales. At this time Julian had an old Morris Oxford saloon which was quite roomy. We had planned to camp that night in the car park opposite the Gorphwysfa Hotel and then to tackle Snowdon the next day via the Crib Goch ridge and Snowdon Horseshow route. This was of course the same route tackled by Mike, Eddie and myself the previous winter leading to the infamous bivouac. However that had been December and this was October with the weather forecast being mild, although wet,

By the time we reached the car park it was dark and raining hard. The decision was made not to even attempt pitching the tent but to try and sleep in the car instead. As Julian had been doing the driving it seemed only fair that he slept on the back seat and I would (attempt to) sleep in the front passenger seat.

It certainly wasn't a comfortable night's 'sleep' but at least it had stopped raining by daybreak. Julian then announced that he always liked to have a cooked breakfast if at all possible and produced a small primus stove which he set up in the front foot well. He then proceeded to cook some kippers on it! The smell was awful and nothing could have induced me to eat any of them, but Julian managed to devour the lot!

It was a great relief to escape from the car and to begin the ascent of Crib Goch, which loomed above us in the mist. Although the rain had stopped the cloud level was persistent above 2,000 feet and the views were generally poor on this, my fifth ascent of Snowdon.

There were few people on the summit and we eventually completed the circuit of the Snowdon Horseshoe and arrived back at the car park in the afternoon. It had now started to rain again in earnest and the decision was made to get a bite to eat at the Gorphwysfa and then to cut our losses and head back to London. This seemed to be a very long journey. It was dark and wet but worse still the car reeked with the smell of kippers!

The day after our return to the hospital I met up with Julian in the Union Bar in Huntley Street. The poor guy looked even more shattered than before his 'relaxing' weekend away in the mountains. Once again my good intentions had been a complete failure!

CHAPTER EIGHT

1968

OBERGURGL REVISITED

By mid-February my six-month house surgeon appointment was coming to an end. I had a new job in the School Dental Service in Hounslow commencing in March. But before this, a group of us had decided to have a skiing holiday before the winter was over. Eddie, Mike and I were going to be joined by Pete F, who had been in our year, and Alfie H, an old school friend of Mike.

The unfortunate and unsuspecting ski resort we

had chosen to visit was to be Obergurgl, which Mike and I had visited the previous summer and which had greatly impressed us. We were also curious as to how it would compare with its summer persona. It was the highest ski resort in the Austrian Tyrol, so good snow was guaranteed for early March.

Pete had skied before, but this was to be a new experience for the rest of us. We discovered that there was a dry ski slope at Crystal Palace and evening classes were available for novices, so we booked ourselves in for three sessions after work. The 'run' consisted of a hillside slope which was covered in lattice matting to simulate a snow slope. Although the run was well floodlit, the main problem was that there were several large trees present on the slope protruding through the latticing, and unfortunately there was no padding present on the trunks. A number of bruising encounters occurred!

Another problem was that at the bottom of the slope there was a large rubber 'arrester' mat. When your skis ran onto the mat you stopped immediately. At least your skis did, but not necessarily you! The general consensus was that surely skiing on snow should be a lot easier. We couldn't wait to get to Obergurgl to try out the real thing.

We travelled by air to Munich and then by coach to Obergurgl. The mountains surrounding the village were reassuringly familiar, but the village itself looked very different under its mantle of snow. We were staying in a hotel not far from the small guest house that Mike and I had stayed in the previous August. We were a little surprised to find that all five of us were sharing the same room, albeit a large one in the basement, somewhat sparsely furnished with a small wash-basin in one corner. Evening meals were provided at a nearby restaurant and we were all soon enjoying a good dinner and a few glasses of wine in preparation for ski school the next morning.

SKIING THRILLS AND SPILLS

The next morning we all reported to ski school where, apart from Pete, we were all enrolled into the beginners' class. The actual skiing itself did not, at least initially, present us with too many problems – after all we were all quite fit young men and the introduction sessions at Crystal Palace proved to be invaluable. At least we could all do snowplough turns and eventually come to a stop!

However, mastering the ski lifts was another matter, especially as far as Eddie was concerned. The first type of lift we encountered was the drag lift, which was basically an inverted T-bar which was dragged up the snow-covered hillside by a continuous cable. The trick was to position yourself so that the T-bar made contact just below your backside and with your skis pointing in a straight line uphill. Then with luck and a following wind you would be smoothly dragged up the mountainside. The problem was that if you let the bar slide down the back of your legs you could be flipped over in a backward somersault!

The best idea was to choose a travelling companion on the other side of your T-bar who was approximately the same height as yourself. However even despite this, Eddie seemed to have a continuing problem with dislodging both himself and whoever was unfortunate enough to be sharing the bar with him. So much so that we all refused to ride with him.

I was following him up on the drag lift one morning when an unsuspecting middle-aged woman was riding with him. As the drag lift took us up and over a steep ridge Eddie fidgeted on the bar and managed to fall off and slide down the hillside to the right. This unbalanced the bar and the poor woman was tipped off the bar and disappeared down the hillside to the left!

After that we thought it might be safer to try him on a chair lift. One afternoon, after ski school, we thought we would take the chair lift up the Festkogel, one of the nearby peaks which Mike and I had climbed the previous summer. I got on the chair in front of Eddie and the plan was for me to turn round and take a photo of him when we were higher up the mountain. When I eventually turned to take the picture I was surprised to see an empty swinging seat behind me! When we eventually met up with him it seemed that he'd sat back too hard in the seat, which had then swung back. When it then tilted forwards again he'd caught the tips of his skis in the snow and had been catapulted forward out of his seat to fall face downwards into the snow. He'd then had to wait until he could safely get out of the way of the succession of chairs coming over the top of him. After that he tried to avoid all lifts as much as possible.

THE SNOWMEN

One of the good things about Obergurgl as a ski resort is that being the highest resort in Austria, there is snow even in the village itself, so that at the end of the day you can ski right up to the door of your hotel. One of the routes through the outskirts of the village went past several barns, outside which there was a group of large snowmen, all six to seven feet tall. They were quite a welcoming sight at the end of a tiring day out on the slopes.

One afternoon our ski instructor, Hans, took us all on a cross-country ski through a nearby forest where there was a spectacular frozen waterfall. We came out of the forest and there looming in the distance was a dramatic snow-covered mountain that looked very familiar to Mike and me. We realised that the peak was our old friend Hangerer, which we had climbed the previous August whilst we had been staying at the Schonweiss Hut. Our companions seemed quite impressed when told of our ascent.

The light was starting to fade as we zoomed confidently through the outskirts of the village back to our hotel, expertly swerving through the group of snowmen. Unfortunately Eddie failed to swerve and managed to ski straight through one of the snowmen, which disintegrated into a heap with him prostrate on the top. It was only when we skied back to Eddie to check if he was all right that we discovered that he was covered in manure! We then realised that the 'snowmen' were in fact heaps of manure from the nearby cowsheds which had become covered with snow. We tried to clean him up as best we could with handfuls of snow, but there was no disguising the unmistakable aroma that lingered around him for days!

ROUND THE BEND

During the second week of our skiing holiday there was a local festival which was being celebrated by a large party of the local inhabitants at the restaurant where we had our evening meal. We naturally joined in with the general joviality of the evening and inevitably seemed to consume a number of bottles of red wine.

We later made our way rather unsteadily down the path back to our hotel. It was freezing hard and there were no street lights, but fortunately lights from the houses lit up the snow-covered track. Several people fell over, but everyone managed to slide or 'toboggan' back to our hotel. Here we all collapsed onto our beds somewhat the worse for wear (or should it be red wine?)

After a while it was discovered that 'someone' had been sick in the basin in the corner of the room, effectively blocking it completely. Being of a practical disposition (probably my Boy Scout training) I managed to find a bucket from somewhere and placed it under the sink. I then managed to unscrew the U-bend so that all of the sink's contents fell down into the bucket. Someone opened the window and, because the room was virtually at ground level, the bucket's contents were thrown out onto the snow. The window was quickly shut as an icy blast was blowing in.

A short time later someone was brushing his teeth utilising the wash basin when he realised that his feet were getting wet! Closer inspection revealed that this was because the U-bend was missing. This discovery resulted in the mass realisation that the U-bend must have been thrown out of the window with the rest of the bucket's contents!

The window was quickly re-opened and there glistening in the snow and vomit was the U-bend. As Eddie was the smallest, we managed to partially lower him out of the window and he managed to retrieve the vital piece of plumbing. This was soon re-connected and normal service was resumed.

We all had a good night's sleep after all that excitement and didn't think any more of the night's events. However after breakfast the Ski Holiday rep paid us a visit to say there had been complaints about the noise from us the night before and if there was any repetition we could be asked to leave! We didn't mention the plumbing incident but we did point out, in our defence, that it was somewhat unrealistic to pack five fellows into one room and not to expect any noise!

Fortunately the rest of our stay was uneventful, mainly due to exhaustion, and we all safely returned back to London. At least no one had suffered any lasting injuries and a good time had been had by all. Obergurgl had proved to be a good ski resort but I think I preferred the summertime as the best season to visit this delightful little Tyrolean village.

RETURN TO THE HIGHLANDS

Back in London changes were afoot. Eddie, Dave W and I moved into a flat in Ealing whilst Mike was far more adventurous and moved to Papua New Guinea. Initially we thought it was because he no longer wished to flat share with us, but it was because he was going to work for the Australian Dental Service and that's where the job was. My new employment was based in Brentford in the wilds of Hounslow working for the School Dental Service. I was fortunate to be seconded for one session a week in the Children's Department back at UCH Dental Hospital. The registrar in the department was Sam R, who had been a student there two years ahead of me. Chatting to Sam it transpired that he was very keen to try some mountaineering and so we started to plan a climbing trip. Julian B was also keen to be included and the fourth member of our team was to be John H, an old school friend of Sam's.

But which mountains were to be fortunate enough to have us tramping over them? I had visited Glen Coe in 1965 with my old school friend Mick and had been very impressed with the climbing potential of the area. If you recall, the weather that August had been dreadful, but this time we were planning to visit in the month of May, which hopefully experienced less rainfall. Also I suggested that we stayed in a guest house instead of camping.

All this planning was a welcome diversion from the day job of acclimatizing to working in a health centre. The dental clinic was in its own wing attached to the main clinic. This seemed to be the usual layout for health centres, as no one apparently wanted dental services anywhere near them!

One morning, at the end of a session, I was sitting in the dental office when I noticed a white switch on the wall. There was no sign or information attached to indicate its function. I asked the dental nurse, but she did not know and thought that it was obsolete. I gave it a firm press but nothing seemed to happen. A few minutes later I commentated to the nurse that a lot of the health centre staff seemed to be standing out in the car park. She didn't know what was going on but I wondered if perhaps someone had a new car and they were all admiring it?

The next moment the office door flew open and the caretaker rushed in brandishing a large fire extinguisher He exclaimed "Where is it?" Upon enquiring what it was he was looking for he shouted "The fire of course. The alarm went off in my office to show there is a fire in Dental!"

He calmed down upon discovering that there was no fire, but then got all excited again upon discovering that I'd only pressed the button out of curiosity. He stomped off muttering to tell the rest of the staff it was only a false alarm and also to say what he thought of young dentists. I was glad that I was going to be away in Scotland for the next couple of weeks!

THE ROAD NORTH

Julian had kindly offered to provide and drive his Morris Oxford car for our Highland trip. I was still in the process of having driving lessons, which I had put off umpteen times during five years of undergraduate training. We were going to meet Sam up in Scotland, as he was having a few days up there on holiday with relatives. So it was just Julian, John H and I who set off to drive from London up to Lincoln to spend the night at Julian's parents' house en route to the north. Fortunately the smell of kippers from our previous Snowdon trip seemed now to have vanished.

Julian's mother gave us a splendid fish pie for supper and after a good night's sleep we were off early the next morning up the A1 northwards to eventually reach Scotch Corner. From there we headed across to Penrith, Carlisle and then on to Glasgow.

In Glasgow we had been kindly invited to spend the night with an old flatmate of mine from our Highbury Fields days. Rodney K was now married and had a position as Lecturer in Chemistry at Glasgow University. Rodney and his wife had quite a small flat but made us very welcome. We offered to get a take-away supper and Rodney said that there was a good fish and chip shop locally albeit in a rather "rough area". We weren't quite sure what he meant by a "rough area" but anyway we drove round to the chippie and Rodney said he would dash in and get the food, while we hovered in the car outside, but we had to make sure that the engine was kept running! Anyway it all went to plan. Rodney dashed out with the food and we safely roared away. All a bit 'Keystone Cops'. We never did find out what would have happened if the car had stalled!

The next day we bade farewell to Rodney and his wife and set off northwards. We drove past Loch Lomond, Tyndrum and Bridge of Orchy (from where Mick and I had caught our homebound train after our previous Glen Coe adventure nearly three years before). We crossed over Rannoch Moor, passed the Kings House Hotel and entered Glen Coe with the majestic Buachaille Etive Mor on our left hand side. We proceeded down the Glen with me pointing out the appetising group of mountains that were awaiting us. The Three Sisters on the left, then the Aonach Eagach ridge on the right and finally the Pap of Glencoe (Sgurr na Ciche) before we drove through the village of

Glencoe and along the side of Loch Leven towards Ballachulish. We were booked into a guest house for the two weeks in Ballachulish, very close to where the car ferry crossed Loch Leven (this was before the bridge was built). Sam had already arrived and was able give us a guided tour and help us to unpack the car.

I was sharing a room with Julian and was somewhat surprised when he took two bricks out of the boot of his car and transported them up to our room. "What on earth are those for? A crude trouser press?" I enquired. Nothing so simple. Julian carefully placed the bricks under the feet at the bottom of his bed. This now meant that the head of the tilted bed was some four inches lower than the foot end. Seeing the look of incredulity on my face, Julian explained that he had always slept with his head lower than his feet so as to ensure a good supply of blood to his brain whilst asleep!

I remained unconvinced of any positive gain from such elevation until I met up with Julian many years later at our old students' '25 years since graduation' party. I gasped in amazement at Julian's hair. Whereas the rest of us were either grey or bald (some partially both) his hair was the same colour and mass that it had been 25 years earlier. His foot-of-the-bed elevation theory had obviously had some positive benefit – too late for me though!

MUNRO BAGGING

My previous experience of Scottish weather a few years earlier had been a very wet one, but our first Highland morning of the 21st May was a bright and sunny one so we were eager to make the most of it while it lasted. A 'Munro' is the name given to a Scottish mountain which is over 3,000 feet and the two peaks to the south of Ballachulish that we climbed that morning, Sgorr Donuill (3,284 feet) and Sgorr Dhearg (3,362 feet), came into that category. We started the ascents just above sea level and certainly felt quite 'stretched' by the end of the day as none of us had carried out any climbing in the previous few months.

Next day we were all feeling rather stiff, so we spent a couple of hours exploring the village of Glencoe. We discovered in one shop some specimens of locally-sourced granite boulders that had been split open to reveal hollow cavities lined with amethysts. The tell-tale signs on the outsides of the boulders were small quartz veins, so we thought we would keep our eyes open for similar specimens.

The following day, the 23rd May, was another gloriously sunny one, so we set ourselves an ambitious route. We drove back down the Glen eastwards and found a small car park on the A82 opposite the Three

Sisters. We crossed the road and followed the sign pointing to the 'Meeting of Three Waters' and walked over the small bridge spanning the River Coe. We then ambled up the track which ran alongside the stream called 'Allt Coire Gabhail' which flowed down towards us between two of the three sisters, Beinn Ffada being the eastern sister with Gearr Aonach the central sibling. (The western sister is Aonach Dubh.) The lower part of the track led up through wooded slopes, criss-crossing the stream. But all of a sudden the trees ended and we found ourselves in the 'Lost Valley', which is essentially a hanging valley left from the era when the glen was gouged out during one of the ice-ages.

There is certainly a magical feel to the 'Lost Valley', which had the impressive backdrop of the snow-capped Bidean nam Bian. It almost felt as if time had stood still and indeed a grazing Brontosaurus would not have seemed out of place.

We climbed up the steep eastern side of the Lost Valley to reach the summit of Beinn Ffada at 3,064 feet. From there we proceeded on to climb Stob Coire Sgreamach (3,497 feet) which means the 'Peak of the Dreadful Corrie'. What a wonderful name! Even in late May there was an invigorating climb along the snow-covered ridge leading up to the summit of Bidean nam Bian (3,766 feet), from which we enjoyed a panorama of wonderful views.

After lunch we climbed Stob Coire nan Lochan at 3,657 feet before descending to the Pass of Glencoe down the valley between Aonach Dubh and Gearr Aonach. Unfortunately we finished up on the western side of the stream draining into the River Coe so we had to wade through the stream and make our way back to the bridge at the 'Meeting of Three Waters'. From there we squelched back to the car.

BIG BEN

On my previous trip to Scotland I had climbed Ben Nevis with Mick S but had been somewhat underwhelmed by the experience, mainly due to the summit being merely the highest point of a plateau. However the lads were keen to climb the highest mountain in the British Isles, so on the 25th of May we set out to do just that. There was a long queue of cars waiting at the Ballachulish Ferry and from the time marker posts we worked out that it would be quicker to drive around the head of Loch Leven. We then drove on to Loch Linnhe and up to Fort William.

We set off up Glen Nevis and then up the long zigzagging track which led eventually to the summit cairn. There was a general feeling of anticlimax with the climb, which certainly did not compare with Bidean nam Bian a few days previously.

We returned to Ballachulish by mid-afternoon and decided to try a bit of rock splitting. Over the previous few days we had collected a number of small granite boulders and thought we would try to split them to see if there were any amethysts inside. This proved to be somewhat problematical as we didn't have a hammer and chisel with us. However in the grounds of the guest house was a small rocky outcrop and we stood on the top of it hurled the boulders down onto some lower rocks. We didn't find any amethysts, indeed we had a problem finding any of the shattered remnants. Our antics did however seem to provide considerable amusement for the other guest house residents.

YET MORE MUNROS

The next day we drove back down the Glen to the car park again opposite the 'Meeting of Three Waters'. We crossed over the River Coe and set off up the Buachaille Etive Beag ridge, which we followed up to the summit of Stob Dubh at 3,219 feet. There we had lunch admiring the views to the south of Glen Etive. (Many years later some of the James Bond film 'Skyfall' was shot in Glen Etive.)

Much to our surprise the sunshine continued the following day and we felt we had to keep climbing before the weather broke. It was the 27th of May and we commenced by climbing the conical Pap of Glencoe (Sgurr na Ciche) above Glencoe village. This was followed by a stiff climb up Sgor nam Fiannaidh (3,168 feet). Next we traversed the dramatic Aonach Eagach ridge (at 3,080 feet). This is one of the four great traverses in the British Isles, the others being the Crib Goch ridge on the Snowdon Horseshoe, Striding Edge leading up to Helvelyn in the Lake District and the Cuillin ridge on the Isle of Skye.

We had lunch on the summit of Meall Dearg (3,118 feet) enjoying the wonderful panorama of Glen Coe below us. We continued on our way eastwards and eventually descended down the Devil's Staircase to the Pass of Glen Coe, down which we wearily trudged back westwards alongside the River Coe. We passed Loch Achtriochtan with the dark slit of Ossian's Cave above and then finally reached Glen Coe village. It had been a long day but a very rewarding one. I had thought that Crib Goch would take a lot of beating as a spectacular ridge traverse but Aonach Eagach is at least its equal.

THE DAM BUILDERS

The next day the sun shone down brightly on us once more. It had been an unbelievable period of good weather in Glen Coe, completely the opposite of my previous experience there. The problem was our bodies needed a day off to recover from climbing mountains. We decided to have a relaxing day spent lazing on the banks of the River Coe. At least that was the theory! We purchased some food and liquid refreshment and found a suitable picnic spot on the south bank of the river more or less opposite the campsite where Mick S and I had nearly been washed away three years earlier. Julian had a book he wanted to read and made himself comfortable sitting under a tree on the river bank. The rest of us fancied something a bit more active and decided to try and build a dam across part of the river.

After a couple of hours 'beavering' we had quite a sizable promontory jutting out into the Coe. Due to the recent dry spell the water flow wasn't too strong and we were able to shift quite a number of large boulders out into the stream. Julian called us ashore for a lunch break, allowing us to admire our handiwork. We wondered how often the Ordnance Survey revised their maps. After lunch we resumed our beaver-like activity and Julian returned to his book. Our construction was now well out into the river and we started to build an arm which ran parallel with the bank. This produced quite a large pool of water, which would have been quite pleasant to swim in if the water temperature had been higher.

Our activities drew quite a bit of interest from passing motorists on the nearby A82. A coach of tourists even stopped at one point. We then used smaller stones to fill in as many gaps as possible and by mid-afternoon felt that our dam building ambitions were now satisfied.

Julian had finished his book and came over to admire our handiwork. He decided that he would perform the 'capping off' ceremony for us and selected a very large flat boulder for the purpose. He staggered with it out to the middle of the dam and ceremoniously dropped it into place. Unfortunately he managed to drop it onto one of his fingers! There was quite a bit of blood coming from a nasty gash from the end of his crushed finger.

We managed to bind up his finger, which staunched the bleeding, and Julian was then able to drive back into the village where the local medical centre was still open. He was duly patched up and we returned to the guest house. Unfortunately Sam was the only other qualified driver amongst us and he wasn't insured to drive Julian's car. A lesson to be learned, always try and have a back-up driver in case of emergencies!

ALL GOOD THINGS...

The next day, the 29th of May, was our last climbing day before returning to London. At last a few clouds were starting to appear in the sky towards the west. Julian was quite happy to drive, following his mishap the day before, and so we headed eastwards down the Glen to Buacchaille Etive Mor (often simply called 'The Beuckle') at the entrance to the Pass of Glen Coe. Here we climbed the northern summit, Stob Dearg, at 3,345 feet. This was to be our final climb and we sat there enjoying the views up the pass. We all agreed what a superb location it had been to spend a climbing holiday. The weather had been perfect and we had managed to climb a total of 12 Munros.

As we picked our way back down to the car the sky became darker and finally the rain started to fall. The holiday was over!

A FAMILY AFFAIR

During the next few months I persevered with learning to drive and finally managed to pass my driving test. Next on the agenda was to acquire a car and I purchased an old Wolseley 16/60 which was quite spacious and had a large boot, ideal for climbing trips. My younger brother Barry thought so too and suggested that I take him and an old school friend of his, Roger T, on a climbing weekend to Wales and perhaps climb Snowdon. He'd listened to all my stories and thought it might be good fun to get in on the action!

The plan was to drive up to Snowdonia and camp in the usual car park at the Gorphwysfa Hotel in the shadow of Crib Goch. We set off on the 27th of September, but the journey along the A5 was very slow in torrential rain. The rain had stopped by the time we crossed into Wales and the light was fading by the time we passed through Betws-y-Coed, so we decided to camp in the first likely-looking spot. We came to a suitable lay-by, parked up and pitched the tent on the grassy verge next to the car. The wind was quite blustery so some of the guy-ropes were anchored onto the car to be on the safe side.

It was rather a squash with the three of us in the tent (I had a flashback to Rod's tent on Scafell Pike). Roger did a 'Titus Oates' offering to leave the tent. Instead he slept in the car and had the best night's sleep of the three of us.

Once the sun was up the next morning we resumed our journey, passing through Capel Curig and onto the Llanberis Pass and finally reached the Gorphwysfa car park. At least the weather was dry albeit rather cloudy. After a quick breakfast we set off up the track leading up to Crib Goch. Barry and Roger were quite fit 18-year-olds and we made good progress. Visibility was reasonable crossing the Crib Goch ridge with intermittent views of Snowdon as we proceeded around the Horseshoe route via Crib-y-Ddysgl. The summit cairn of Snowdon was reached without incident (my sixth visit) and as we had made good progress there were only a few other people sharing the view with us. Some threatening clouds were approaching from the west so we kept on going around the Horseshoe before descending to Llyn Llydaw. We reached the car just as rain was setting in.

No one fancied the prospect of another night in the tent or car and the decision was made to drive back to Northampton. Although we had achieved our objective of climbing Snowdon I didn't think that either of the lads was that enamoured with climbing because they never asked to come again!

THERE'LL BE A WELCOME ON THE HILLSIDES

No sooner had Sam and Julian heard of my trip to Snowdonia than they were hinting at another trip to include them. We all felt that we'd had enough of 'camping' in either tents or cars and perhaps a local inn might be a good idea, especially as the autumn was upon us. We managed to arrange for a few nights stay in an inn in Beddgelert, which also had the advantage that meals were also available. I also offered the use of my car and limited driving experience which was accepted!

Our journey up to Snowdonia was fortunately lacking in excitement and the accommodation was found to be very acceptable.

The next morning, the 26th of October, saw us toiling up Tryfan, this was the second time for Julian but a new summit for Sam. There were very few other climbers around on Tryfan and later on we had the Glyders and Bristly Ridge to ourselves. We descended past the Devil's Kitchen and Llyn Idwal on our way back to the car.

That night at the inn we had a good dinner and then were entertained to an evening of song from the locals which went on long into the night. Too long in fact as it eventually delayed us getting to sleep upstairs!

It seemed strange the next morning to be driving into the Gorphwysfa car park again, it was only four weeks since my last visit there. Crib Goch was becoming quite familiar to me by now, also it was virtually a year to the day that Julian had last been there with me (that was after he'd cooked the kippers in his car). Crib-y-Ddysgl came and went in the mist and soon we were all standing on the summit of

Snowdon. Visibility was disappointing again, always a potential problem on mountains in Snowdonia, the Lake District and also the Grampians, as there is a large amount of water westwards!

We continued our route around the Horseshoe and descended back to the car park.

We enjoyed a good meal at the inn again and fortunately this time a quieter evening. The next day was rather wet but we had a more or less uneventful journey back to London except for one exciting aquaplane in the fast lane on the M1. All good experience!

CHAPTER NINE

1969

ON A CLEAR DAY...

The beginning of the new year saw Sam, Julian and me back in Snowdonia. It seemed a good way to start 1969. I think, on reflection, that the three of us had now become addicted to the Snowdon Horseshoe.

After the success of our previous visit we decided to stay again at the inn in Beddgelert. We had a good journey from London and the weather forecast looked good. So it was that on the 11th of January the three of us found ourselves approaching the summit of Crib Goch once more.

From the car park below it appeared that once more the tops of the surrounding peaks were covered in cloud. However once above 2,000 feet we found that the clouds and mist were absent. By the time we reached the summit of Crib Goch an incredible vista opened up before us. The whole of the Snowdon Horseshoe above 2,000 feet was standing there clear in the sunshine, looking like a Pacific atoll with the well-demarcated cloud level below us looking like a surrounding ocean.

Our cameras started to work overtime, all the way along the Crib Goch ridge up to the summit of Snowdon itself. This was my eighth visit and I had never seen it as amazing as this. There was a mantle of snow over the whole of the Snowdon Horseshoe giving a magical feel to the mountain. We all felt that this was what mountaineering was all about.

Another bonus was that, apart from a handful of other mountaineers, we virtually had Snowdon to ourselves. Wintertime seemed to be the best time to climb here, provided one was properly prepared and equipped!

The next day we climbed Tryfan, which was a bit of an anticlimax as there was more mist and less snow in comparison. However the memories of that day on Snowdon have persisted for many years, thanks to the photographs we managed to take.

FLYING THE FLAG

Eddie P, one of the original 'Snowdon Survivors', had gone out to Rhodesia in the late summer of 1968 to work in a dental practice in Salisbury. I had written to Eddie just after Christmas to enquire how he was getting on and filling him in with our latest climbing exploits. In Rhodesia in the September of 1968 the Rhodesian High Court ruled that the Prime Minister Ian Smith's government was that of Rhodesia. To mark this event a new Rhodesian flag was created. In my letter to Eddie I had, somewhat tongue in cheek, suggested to him that if he sent me one of these new flags then we would plant it on the top of Snowdon the next time we were up there to celebrate our survival on that mountain.

Much to my surprise, in February I received a package from Eddie which had a Customs label on it describing the contents as a 'souvenir table cloth'. It was of course the new Rhodesian flag! Sam and Julian didn't need much encouragement for us to organise another trip to Snowdonia. Another ex-UCH dental student and a flatmate of Julian's called John T was very keen to come on one of our climbing trips, although he had no previous mountaineering experience. A weekend in mid-March was planned for our next trip and we duly booked into the Beddgelert inn, which was proving to be a popular base.

So on the morning of the 15th of March the four of us set off from the Gorphwysfa car park to tackle Snowdon once more. The whole of the Horseshoe was covered in snow, and because there was a novice amongst us we decided that instead of the usual Crib Goch route we would make our ascent by the easier Pyg Track. This passes to the north of Llyn Llydaw and Glaslyn before ascending relatively easily up to the ridge between Crib-y-Ddysgl and the summit of Snowdon.

Fortunately there were only a few climbers on the Snowdon summit when we reached it. I tied the Rhodesian flag onto the shaft of my ice axe and then posed with it resting on top of the summit cairn in best Ed Hillary fashion. Photos were taken so that a copy could be sent to Eddie to prove that his flag had been put to good use.

We then made our descent back down the Pyg Track, unintentionally quite rapid on one section. We spent a convivial evening back at the inn celebrating John T's initiation into our mountaineering fraternity.

WHAT GOES AROUND COMES AROUND

The next morning we drove northwards to Llyn Ogwen, where we parked the car and headed up to Llyn Idwal with the object of first climbing Glyder

Fawr, then going along the Bristly Ridge to Glyder Fach. Above Llyn Idwal the snow covered mountainside proved to be very icy, so I put on my crampons and went ahead with my ice axe, chipping out steps where necessary. I had a spare pair of old ex-WD crampons which I lent to Sam, who proceeded to crunch along quite happily. The steep slope started to level out, but then unfortunately a thick swirling mist descended and we found ourselves in a virtual white-out situation, when you lose sight of any horizons and can become quite disorientated. Fortunately I had a set of previously-noted compass bearings and distances for such an eventuality, and so we set off on the first bearing.

It was then that the strap on Sam's left crampon broke, so he had to remove it. He found that he could move along fairly well by 'clomping' down with the crampon on his right foot and sliding his left foot along behind. After about 10 minutes, when I calculated a change in compass bearing was due, we had a brief refreshment stop to eat some fruit cake. Sam had his anorak hood tied tightly under his chin and couldn't get his mouth open far enough to push the cake in, with the result he left a pile of cake crumbs behind in the snow.

We set off once more into the all-enveloping white mist. After another half hour of walking I was starting to get concerned that our route was still undulating, as it should by now have flattened out on top of the Glyders plateau. It was then that we noticed another set of tracks in the snow, apparently going in the same direction. Sam then discovered that one set of prints also seemed to be of someone else walking along wearing only one crampon! Sam was obviously a trendsetter. However, a minute later we came across a pile of cake crumbs in the snow...

Everyone turned around to look at me. How had we been walking round in a circle for an hour? I looked closely at my Silva compass once more and then realised with horror that it had somehow filled with water, which must then have frozen. Where were we?

By continuing uphill, we eventually seemed to reach a flatter area which must have been the broad Glyder ridge. Unexpectedly, we then came up against a pile of vertical slabs. The only way appeared to be up and over. After ten minutes scrambling up icy rocks we seemed to have reached the top of a pinnacle. At this moment a breeze stirred the mist, everything became lighter and within a minute the mist had lifted to reveal a bright blue sky.

We looked around in amazement to discover that indeed we were standing on top of a pinnacle. The only thing was that this pinnacle was sitting alone on a plateau with at least a hundred feet all around it. We could have just bypassed it! We all quickly scrambled down before anyone came along and wondered what we were all doing standing Nelson-like on top of a column. We continued over Glyder Fawr and then Glyder Fach before descending without further deviation back to Llyn Ogwen and the car.

The next day we returned to London without the need for compass bearings! As soon as possible I went and purchased an oil-filled Silva compass, which shouldn't freeze. I then posted a copy of the flag-planting ceremony on Snowdon to Eddie to prove that the task had been completed.

READ ALL ABOUT IT!

It was just over three weeks later that I received another package from Rhodesia. This time it contained a copy of the *Rhodesian Herald*, Salisbury, dated the 10th April 1969. Why on earth was Eddie sending me a newspaper? Then – shock and horror! There on the front page was the picture of me holding the new Rhodesian flag on the top of Snowdon. I was described as 'a keen mountain climber from Northampton' and the other three lads were all mentioned by name as well. The picture was accompanied by a short story of how the flag came to be there. Fortunately there was no mention of our professions, nor indeed of Eddie's.

I immediately let the others know what had happened and we all waited in some trepidation over the next few weeks in case any of us had a visitation from the Foreign Office or any enquiry from our own regulatory body. Fortunately all remained quiet, but we resolved to keep a lower profile in the future, especially as far as Eddie was concerned!

THE WANDERER RETURNS

Just after Easter Mike returned from Papua New Guinea. It was getting on for nearly two years since he had been climbing with us lads and he was anxious to make up for lost time. I had just started working in a dental practice in Leytonstone which belonged to Chris L, who had been in our year. Mike and I had arranged to meet up in the UCH Union in Huntley Street one evening after work. Over a few beers we caught up on what we had both been up to over the last year, the skiing holiday to Obergurgl having been our last mutual trip. Mike realised that the Festkogel was the last mountain we had climbed together, in August 1967.

We decided that a return trip to Austria was indicated for the forthcoming summer holidays. I had the latest newsletter from the Austrian Alpine Club (AAC) and we thought we would try one of their guided tours. How it worked was that one of the AAC's guides would lead a party of three climbers during the week and provide guidance and advice on Alpine techniques. It sounded ideal – we just needed another climber to make up the team. Julian and Sam weren't interested in Alpine climbing but John H, who had come on the Scotland trip the previous year, was keen to join us and so we contacted the AAC and arrangements were made for August.

Mike felt that a few days' climbing in Snowdonia in the interim would be a good idea to try and get him fit, also to see if he could remember how to tie any of the knots! Julian and Sam were keen to come along as well and our usual accommodation was booked in Beddgelert. Mike was quite impressed that we now stayed at an inn on our climbing trips.

So it felt very like old times on a sunny morning in June when all four of us stood on the top of Tryfan gazing down along the Nant Ffrancon Pass. By midday as we climbed up Glyder Fach we were all feeling rather hot, but there was quite a welcome breeze along the Bristly Ridge as we approached Glyder Fawr. On the descent we had a welcome cooling paddle on the shore of Llyn Idwal.

We all slept well that night and because another hot day was predicted an early start was made the next morning, the 14th of June. The sun was making itself felt by the time we reached the top of Crib Goch, but at least we knew the majority of height had been gained by that point. The view from Crib Goch was very unusual as far as we were concerned. Not a cloud in sight!

The perfect weather continued as we progressed around the Horseshoe, over Crib-y-Ddysgl and onto the Snowdon summit for the third time that year. In total this was my tenth ascent of Snowdon and had provided the best views ever. I think Mike was a bit disappointed that we didn't have another flag to plant on the summit! At least the weather and views helped to make up for it.

Once again Snowdonia and its mountains had provided a good battery recharge, all in readiness for the next Alpine challenge.

RETURN TO THE ALPS

July was a busy month spent preparing for our return to Austria later in August. The Austrian Alpine Club had supplied us with a list of equipment which we had to take on the trip. We already had ice axes, crampons and climbing helmets. The 'English' climbing harness at the time was a 'waistband' made up of 4-5 loops of No.1 rope. The AAC harness was made using a length of No.3 rope and worn over the chest and shoulders. There were instructions for how this was to be constructed and which knots to use. Unfortunately, this meant having to try and teach Mike yet again how to tie bowline and reef knots!

It didn't get any easier. Our loaded rucksacks were supposed to be below 35lbs as we would be travelling between the higher huts with all our gear, including ropes. We were advised not to have down sleeping bags, due to weight and space, but just to carry 'sheet' sleeping bags as blankets would be provided at the huts.

The week before we were due to head off to Austria, the weather in London was beginning to get hotter and hotter, and the working conditions in the Leytonstone practice were becoming unbearable. The surgery window wouldn't open and there was no air conditioning. The dental unit itself was quite old; it appeared to have been made in Japan in the early part of the 20th century. There were a number of buttons and switches on the back of the unit, but most of them appeared to be corroded and none of them were labelled. On the top of the unit was an enormous three-bladed fan, which Chris had said did not work.

At the end of my last working day before our holiday, I was treating Mrs D, who started to complain of feeling very hot and pleaded with me to switch the unit's fan on. I found a somewhat rusty switch protruding from the top of the unit. I clicked it one way, but nothing happened. I then clicked it the other way, but still nothing. One final attempt and the switch broke off! So that was that. However, a rumbling noise then started down in the bowels of the unit and slowly the fan started to turn with a creaking noise. Gradually the fan started to turn faster and the creaking noise changed into a loud grating whir.

As the fan went faster the unit itself started to shake. At this point I realised the unit was not bolted to the floor and it started to creep towards the dental chair as the whine from the fan became ear-splitting. Mrs D screamed and leapt from the chair as I rushed to the fuse box and switched off the power. Mrs D was re-booked for a few weeks later, by which time the unit would be repaired. It also gave me time to recover – and what could be better than recuperating in the Austrian Alps?

The next day we were on a coach heading towards the continent. In 1969 the AAC arranged coach travel to the Tyrol instead of using the trains. The seats were specially constructed so that when the coach stopped for the passengers' evening meal, the seats were somehow realigned to form upper and lower couchettes. It was all very clever but at 6 foot 4 inches I didn't fit very well into the 'sleeping' space. As a result I didn't get much sleep!

Our destination was the Zillertal Alpen region and when we eventually reached our destination we were met by the AAC guides who would be our mountaineering mentors for the next week. One of our guides was a young Austrian, only a few years older than we were, called Peter Habeler. He was accompanied by an older colleague called Tony Vogler. Besides the three of us there were another three lads who made up the rest of our party.

We set off in a minibus to a higher village deeper into the Zillertal Alps. From there we sent off on foot up a steep track to the AAC hut which would be our base for the next few days. At the hut we were all supplied with blankets and allocated a Matratzenlager. We were puzzled by the lettering on one side of the blankets. They were inscribed by the words 'fusse-ende'. Our comprehension of German was still lamentable but we eventually translated it as "foot end'. So best to keep your face away from that end of the blanket!

Once we had sorted that out we all slept soundly, making up for the night spent on the coach.

ALPINE DAYS

Early the next morning we went down to the dining room, where we were able to purchase our breakfasts from the serving hatch at the far end. The three of us had worked out that coffee was "Kaffee" (pretty obvious), bread was "Brot", cheese was "Käse" and three was "drei". Mike and John had delegated me to go and order our breakfasts. I went and joined the breakfast queue and when my turn came I stepped forward confidently to the hatch and nonchalantly asked for "drei Kaffee, drei Brot und drei Käse, bitte". The guy at the serving hatch smiled and said "Drei Fruhstück?" This immediately threw me into confusion. What on earth was "Frühstück?" I remembered that when hiking through the Black Forest with the Scouts we had been given some strange rectangular sausages which were highly spiced and incredibly tough to chew. I seemed to remember that they had been called 'Frühstück'. So as to be on the safe side I said, quite emphatically "Nein Frühstück". I then repeated "drei Kaffee, drei Brot und drei Käse, bitte".

The fellow at the serving hatch was getting a bit agitated for some reason. "Ja,ja, drei Frühstück!" he repeated. I was now starting to get a bit perplexed. Why on earth was he carrying on about this Frühstück? Perhaps he'd over-ordered it and was trying to get rid of it? Perhaps it was going off? Anyway I defiantly stood my ground. "Nein Frühstück! Drei Kaffee, drei Brot und drei Käse, BITTE!"

It was then I noticed that the guy standing behind in the queue had collapsed and was lying on his back on the floor shaking uncontrollably. I was just about to launch into first aid mode and move him into the three-quarter prone position when I realised that he was laughing, as were the rest of the people in the queue. "You pillock!" he spluttered. I then discovered that he was one of my countrymen. "Frühstück means breakfast, and that includes coffee, bread and cheese!" We should have taken a dictionary with us.

Once breakfast was finally out of the way our party set off. It was still dark and the air was very cold. As dawn broke the surrounding peaks appeared to be initially bathed in a blue light which gradually took on a more rosy hue as the sun rose.

Our objective was the Gefrorne Wandspitze (10,820 feet) and we climbed in two ropes. Mike, John and I climbed with Tony while the other three climbed with Peter.

Unfortunately the fine start didn't last for long and cloud was bubbling up by the time we reached the summit. But our rope handling skills greatly improved as the day progressed, and even Mike managed to tie his knots.

A convivial evening was spent back in the hut while a storm raged outside. Just as well we weren't camping. Unfortunately the weather hadn't improved by the next morning and the day was spent in the hut chatting to our guides and playing cards. We turned in early, hoping for an early start next day if the weather had improved.

OLPERER

We were up early on the 20th August in the hope that there would be a break in the weather. After a quick Frühstück (!) we had a recce outside and the signs were favourable, so we were soon on our way. Our target was Olperer, the highest peak in the Zillertal Alpen and the 23rd highest in Austria. After the previous day's inactivity it felt good to be climbing again and steady progress was made. The early morning air was cold and still and the only sound was the crunch of our steps on the crisp snow.

Part of our route up Olperer involved ascending the glacier that led up towards the summit. To get onto the glacier involved crossing over a bergschrund (which is a crevasse between the adjacent rock face and the glacier) by a snow bridge. Half the party had crossed without incident and then it was my turn.

I was halfway across the snow bridge when it happened. My right foot suddenly went through the bridge, followed by the whole of my right leg. I whacked the pick of my ice-axe into the snow as far ahead as I could reach and spread-eagled myself on the bridge as much as possible to spread my weight over the greatest surface area. Then I just lay there, hardly daring to breathe.

My companions shouted out "Don't move!" but I hardly needed telling. I lay there for what seemed an eternity expecting the bridge to suddenly give way and me plunging into the depths of the crevasse. Still I couldn't stay there forever, so I very gingerly started to extricate my right leg whilst still trying to keep as spread-eagled as possible. Once extricated I started to crawl/wriggle over the remaining section of the bridge to finally reach the relative safety of the glacier. I think we were all in a state of shock.

The remaining members of the party then continued further up the ridge until a safe crossing point could be found to access the glacier. The party was reunited for the final push to the summit of Olperer at 11,420 feet, where we had a well-earned rest which gave us all, and me especially, time to recover.

We descended by a different and safer route, and Peter taught us how to descend a snow field fast and safely. Indeed Peter was also an expert in glissading. (In 1978 Peter Habeler and Reinhold Messner became the first men to climb Mt Everest without the use of artificial oxygen. Peter Habeler then set the world record for the descent from the summit of Mt Everest to the South Col, completing it in one hour).

To complete our learning experiences for the day our guides gave us a demonstration of how to carry out a crevasse rescue. I was relieved that it was Tony V whom we 'rescued' from the crevasse and not me!

It had been quite a day.

Olperer proved to be the high point of our trip, quite literally. Snow started to fall steadily the next day and kept going, on and off, for the next week. We had to bid farewell to Peter and Tony without managing to do any further climbing. We met up with Peter the next year when he came to visit London to give a talk to the British section of the AAC.

We were already looking ahead to the next year for a return to the Austrian Tyrol. We also resolved that before then we needed to obtain a German dictionary!

CHAPTER TEN

1970
MORE SNOW IN
SNOWDONIA

It was the beginning of the New Year and I had met
up with Sam in the UCH Union bar after work. Sam
was coming to the end of his contract as Registrar in
Paediatric Dentistry at the hospital and was
considering going into general practice in Kent,
whereas I was still in general practice and thinking
about returning to paediatric dentistry. Sam suggested

that I should think about applying for his post at the Dental Hospital.

With all this job uncertainty we thought that we should arrange another climbing trip to Snowdonia as soon as possible, certainly before the snows melted. John H and Mike were keen to join us, as was Mike's old school friend Alfie, who had accompanied us skiing in Obergurgl, and wanted to try some climbing.

Our usual accommodation in Beddgelert was duly booked and so on the 12th of February we found ourselves high up in the Nant Ffrancon Pass battling against a very strong head wind as we approached the summit of Y Garn (3,104 feet). The snow was drifting, which made progress slow but helped to stop us being blown over. That evening we planned the next day's climb up Snowdon. Due to the considerable depth of snow in the area and Alfie's lack of climbing experience it was decided to make the ascent via the less exposed Pyg Track route.

The weather on the 13th of February was perfect, the sky was clear and the Snowdon massif looked spectacular with its Alpine appearance. Some impressive photographs were taken that day. Steady progress was made up the Pyg Track until the final steep section was reached which led up to the ridge where the track joined the Horseshoe route, coming from the right, for the final ascent to the summit.

The snow face here was quite steep and frozen hard. I used my ice-axe to cut hand and foot holds and eventually the whole party made it up to the ridge. More spectacular views were awaiting us looking across to the Snowdon summit. We completed the route up to the top, where we had the summit cairn to ourselves. It was certainly worthwhile climbing Snowdon in the winter months; the views seemed to get better the more times the mountain was climbed (this was my 11th visit).

We went down the way we had ascended, but for safety we roped up to descend the steep section where the holds had been cut. Alfie thoroughly enjoyed the day, and felt he was a real mountaineer now.

On the third day we took Alfie up Glyder Fach and along the Bristly Ridge to Glyder Fawr. Here we were met with an incredible sight. All the rock pinnacles were encased with snow, looking like giant white stalagmites – we might have been on a different planet. Even more spectacular were the giant raised snow footprints which marched across the scene, disappearing into the distance. It appeared that initially the footprints must have been made whilst the snow was soft. The snow around the compressed prints must have been blown away and the remaining 'prints' had then been frozen solid, leaving the prints looking like stepping stones. Our cameras were working overtime again.

These few days in Snowdonia had provided us with the most spectacular 'Alpine' views and photographs that we had ever seen anywhere. It made returning to the Metropolis even more difficult.

I met up with Sam the following week to compare our Snowdonia photographs. He had found a dental practice locally to where he lived and was due to start there in April. I was able to tell him that I also had a new job which was commencing on April the 1st. His old job!

ALL WORK AND NO PLAY

The summer of 1970 proved to be challenging work-wise for all of us would-be mountaineers. I was settling into my new job in the Children's Department at the Dental Hospital. It felt very strange being back at my alma mater but now as a member of staff. Not only did I have my own clinical workload, I also took part in the student teaching. New relationships were being forged with colleagues, especially with the secretary to the Orthodontic Department! Mike was in the process of trying to sort out a degree course in marine biology at Bangor and Sam was settling into general practice. Julian had moved from London; in fact I had moved into his old flat in Chalk Farm.

Trying to organise another climbing trip was

proving difficult but finally Mike, John H and I managed to get together to carry out some planning. We studied the latest Austrian Alpine Club information and decided that we would follow one of their planned itineraries, but instead of using their guides we would go independent, just using the AAC huts. We felt reasonably confident, with the experience gained the previous summer, that we could do our own thing now. The intention was to spend the first part of the trip in the Stubai Alpen and then move onto the Otztaler Alpen, where we hoped to climb the Wildspitze, the highest mountain in the Austrian Tyrol (and the second highest in the whole of Austria). That was the plan anyway!

Arranging a mutually convenient time for our trip proved difficult especially as I was unable to take leave during August due to all the academic staff being away. Eventually we settled for early September and the travel arrangements were made with the AAC. Fortunately for us tall people they had stopped using the long-distance coaches and were using the railways again for transport.

THE STUBAI ALPEN

Our journey to Austria had been uneventful, and it was so much more comfortable by train. The uneventful bit stopped when we caught a small bus to take us up to a village nestling in the Stubai Alpen from which we would walk up to our first hut. We had to load up our rucksacks onto the roof-rack of the bus. A few days before leaving London I had taken my ice axe into one of the prosthetic labs in the Hospital and had ground the blade to a knife-edge. In the act of heaving my rucksack up onto the roof I somehow managed to inflict a deep gash in my left thumb. It bled quite profusely, but we managed to staunch the flow with a handkerchief. By the time we clambered onto the bus, there was standing room only.

Now although I didn't have a problem with other people's blood (just as well being a dentist) the sight of my own tended to make me feel faint. After a few minutes I was starting to feel queasy, then the tunnel vision and white dancing spots started. I said to the other two that I needed to lie down before I passed out. Now that was not easy, as the bus was so crowded and we still couldn't speak German. Eventually I managed to lie down on the bus floor between all the feet with my bloodstained thumb held up in the air. The white spots gradually disappeared, my vision cleared and I could see a dozen faces all looking down at me.

I was quite glad when the bus reached our destination and we set off up a steep track through the foothills to our first hut. That evening we got to know another British party who were on the AAC guided tour on the route that we were intending to follow.

The next day we were going to climb the Ruderhof Spitze. Mike, John and I decided that we would delay our start the next morning for an hour after the other party had left. This would enable us to see the correct route and to give them some space.

THE RUDERHOF SPITZE

The next morning, the 8th of September, we carried out our cunning plan. Following a leisurely breakfast, we periodically wandered outside to monitor the other party's progress up towards the head of the valley. Their progress appeared to be quite slow, possibly not helped by the fact that we would all be carrying full kit that day as that night was to be spent in another hut in the next valley. We delayed for an hour before setting off up the valley in pursuit.

We eventually reached the snowfield which led upwards to the Ruderhof Spitze summit and found en route the rucksacks of the other party. They had obviously left their gear behind in order to travel light for their final climb up to the summit. We found a discreet spot behind an outcrop to leave our rucksacks before continuing the ascent just with ropes and ice-axes.

We hadn't gone very far before we met the other party coming back down. They seemed quite surprised to see us and not at all pleased, as they seemed to guess that we were following them, albeit at a discreet distance.

When we reached the summit of the Ruderhof Spitze (at 11,395 feet the 24th highest peak in Austria) we decided that we would have our lunch there and delay our descent for an hour to let the other party get well ahead of us, especially as we knew we would all be staying at the same hut that evening.

We therefore stayed on the summit longer than we intended and it was well after midday by the time we started to descend. We came to the top of the steep snow field and started to descend in a line abreast. Mike was on one flank, I was in the middle and John H on the other flank. I was descending rapidly in true Habeler style when I was suddenly aware that the centre of the slope had become transformed into a heaving river of snow that was quickly going downhill. It was a slab avalanche!

Mike and John both managed to escape sideways, but I was carried away in the middle. A statistic flashed through my mind – 70% of avalanche deaths are caused by suffocation under the snow! I tried to curl up my body in the shape of a boat. I lay on my back, curled up, feet first, knees bent and holding my ice-axe tightly under my knees. My 'boat' bobbed along at a steady rate down the mountainside with me keeping on top of the river of snow.

After a few hundred feet the slope began to gradually level out and the river of snow and my 'boat' slowed to a halt. I looked back up the mountainside to the two distant figures of my companions high above. I staggered to my feet and waved to show that I was all right. They then both started to slowly descend taking rather circuitous routes.

Some twenty minutes later they joined me, by which time I had managed to remove all the snow that seemed to have penetrated everywhere. Up my trousers, my shirt, my nose and even in my ears! "What kept you both?" I enquired.

We collected our rucksacks and proceeded on to the next AAC hut, even catching up one of the other party en route. The hut was quite spacious and we managed to have our own Matratzenlager. One of the other party spoke to John H in the washroom and asked if we intended to follow them the next day up the Zuckerhuetl. That had been our intention, but we decided that it might be a good idea to perhaps choose a different climb for the next day.

DOWN THE TUBE

We avoided the other party the next morning, enjoying a leisurely breakfast. It also gave us a chance to explore the hut and its 'amenities'. In the passageway outside the lavatories was a large tap with a sign above it proclaiming 'Keine Trinkenwasser'. There was a bucket nearby. The lavatories were non-flushing in the conventional sense. The seat was positioned over the end of a large metal tube which apparently exited via the rear of the hut. The theory was after using the lavatory one followed up by emptying a bucket of water down the tube. Simple but effective!

We also assumed that Trinkenwasser meant drinking water, so we filled up our water bottles. We then set out to climb one of the local peaks called the Gros Trogler Spitze (9,521 feet). The weather was good and we enjoyed some splendid views from the summit, especially looking down on a nearby glacier and its impressive crevasse system.

We returned to the hut by a circuitous route in the mid-afternoon. We were intrigued to see a quite luxuriant shrubbery growing on the far side of the hut, quite out of place on a relatively barren mountainside. Upon further investigation we then saw that the 'loo tubes' emptied out onto that side hence the plant proliferation! It also served as a warning not to go wandering around the backs of mountain huts.

We turned in after supper as we needed a good night's sleep prior to an early start the next day to tackle the Zuckerhuetl.

THE ZUCKERHUETL

The next morning, the 10th of September, we set off at daybreak heading towards the Zuckerhuetl, the highest peak in the Stubai Alpen and the 15th highest in Austria. Unfortunately the weather had deteriorated overnight and there were now fast, low scudding clouds.

The Zuckerhuetl appeared to be quite a popular mountain and there were a number of climbing parties picking their way across the glacier leading up to the main ridge which led up to the summit. This narrowed down to a knife-edge ridge which was only about six inches wide, covered in ice, with impressive drops either side which disappeared into a layer of cloud beneath. This section of ridge was about 200 yards long and had about a one in three incline.

We put on our crampons, roped up and were ready to tackle the ridge. The problem was that there were already three roped-up parties ahead of us ascending the ridge, each with about six or seven climbers per team, and they were all moving incredibly slowly! What we wanted to avoid was to get delayed in the middle of a very exposed ridge.

We took up our position at the start of the ridge and waited for the party in front of us to clear the exposed section before we started, as we were confident we would quickly make the traverse – another advantage of being a three-man team. The ridge was very icy with nothing to belay on to. The problem would come if we all fell off on the same side. We worked out a cunning plan. Mike would lead and I would be in the middle as the heaviest with John H at the rear. If Mike slid off the ridge to the right, I would leap off to the left and slam my ice-axe pick into the ice and behind me John H would jump off right and likewise anchor. The important thing was that we didn't all leap off the same side!

At this point another large party came up behind us and probably wondered why we were just standing there! Fortunately the group in front of us had now cleared the ridge and so we set off. We made steady progress across the ridge without mishap. In fact when we had cleared the ridge section and looked back the party behind only appeared to have made a few feet.

We were soon sitting on top of the Zuckerhuetl (at 11,520 feet) and decided to have our lunch there, which would hopefully allow the 'local traffic' hold-ups to clear. Our concern was what would happen if a group was trying to descend the ridge at the same time that another group was trying to ascend. It really needed one of those roadworks traffic light systems.

Fortunately, by the time we had finished our lunch, all the other groups had gone down and there were no other parties coming up. We descended at our leisure with the additional bonus that the clouds were now clearing, allowing us to enjoy a dramatic Alpine sunset when we had returned to the hut.

TRINKENWASSER

Our ascent of the Zuckerhuetl completed the list of peaks we had wanted to climb in the Stubai and we were now going to move on to the Otztaler Alpen, following the route described in the AAC itinerary. The next hut we stayed in was the remotest that we had so far come across in Austria. We had reached it via a high pass, and it was situated on a rocky outcrop on the edge of a glacier. In fact it was so remote that we were the only ones staying there that night, us and the hut warden. Apparently another party of English climbers had left that morning; they must have been our 'friends' from the Ruderhof Spitze, who were a day ahead of us.

After supper we were settling down in front of the fire in the small dining area and thought a beer would be a good idea, so I said to the warden "Drei bier bitte", to which he replied with an apologetic shrug, "Keine bier". To our consternation we then realised that 'keine' must mean 'no' and that the beer stock had all been drunk by our compatriots! This also meant that the 'Keine Trinkenwasser' that we had been drinking for the last few days was obviously unfit for human consumption!

The warden thought that our consternation was due to his news that there was no beer and he kindly offered to make us some glühwein (mulled wine) in recompense. There was a small stove in the corner of the dining room. He placed a large saucepan on it and poured in a couple of bottles of red wine. For the next half hour he crouched over his saucepan, stirring and adding various spices, all this accompanied by muttered 'incantations'.

Whilst this was going on there was a violent electrical storm raging outside. Thunder and lightning surrounded the hut on its little outcrop. Every now and then a bell in the corner of the room would ring eerily. Apparently this bell was connected to the phone line which ran down to the village in the valley far below. The electrical discharges from the storm were causing it to ring.

Eventually 'Merlin' in the corner of the room, had finished his incantations and we were invited to try his brew. It was very good. We certainly slept well that night, despite the storm outside.

The next day we continued on our way into the Otztaler Alpen and eventually made our way up to the next hut from which we would set out to climb our ultimate mountain, the Wildspitze.

THE WILDSPITZE

Dawn was just breaking on September the 14th when we set out from the hut. The sky was completely cloud free, but it was very cold. It was also very quiet; the only sound was from our boots crunching into the frozen snow. We couldn't see any climbers ahead of us as we started on a zig-zag route up the steep snowfield ahead.

An hour or so later we climbed over a ridge and the summit of the Wildspitze came into sight. We saw that there was a party some way ahead of us on the final ridge section. We encountered a lot of ice covering the rocks and had to stop to put on crampons. We then made faster progress and caught up with the party ahead. Then however the ice petered out and we were back on bare rock, so we had to stop to take off our crampons.

Very soon we were standing on the top of the Wildspitze, at 12,382 feet the second highest peak in Austria. It was the first time we had climbed over twelve thousand feet.

Fittingly the weather was perfect, still cloudless and the views were magnificent. We had lunch and then reluctantly started to make our descent. This proved to be quite uneventful, only punctuated by photo stops.

Climbing the Wildspitze made a fitting end to our Tyrolean holiday. We spent a couple of days in Mayrhofen unwinding before the journey back to London.

EPILOGUE

It has now been over forty years since I returned from climbing the Wildspitze. None of us realised it at the time, but it was to be the last mountain my friends and I would climb together. My decade of mountaineering was over.

In retrospect it had all played a significant part in my life and probably in the lives of all my friends who had accompanied me on all our adventures. Certainly during our student days our climbing excursions had acted as valuable diversions and allowed the recharging of batteries.

Fortunately, despite a few near misses, I survived to tell the tale. I hope that you have enjoyed it.

And what of the mountain men themselves in the post-sixties era? Did we all hang up our ice-axes and crampons? The answer would seem to be yes. We all became respectable married men, settled into our careers, turned into law-abiding citizens and raised families. Mike and Eddie both spent many years working in southern Africa.

Even I didn't return to the mountains for many years, until 2009, when I took my wife Marilyn up to the Lake District for a little 'walking' holiday. I had equipped her with some hiking boots and the intention was to stroll around a few lakes. We stayed at a small guest house at Portinscale, near Keswick, at the head of Derwent Water. The view from our bedroom window was dominated by the looming mass of Skiddaw and there seemed to be a celestial finger beckoning me towards it. Marilyn had never climbed a mountain before, but I found a local guide book which reassuringly said that the mountain was 'grandmother friendly'.

The subsequent ascent the next day was quite long, hot and arduous. Marilyn seemed to have the idea that there was a café at the top and there was a good chance that Ben Fogle himself might be there. I felt it best not to dispel either of these hopes.

Eventually we stood triumphant on the summit of Skiddaw at 3,053 feet. I then felt able to tell her that she had just climbed the fourth highest mountain in England. As far as Ben Fogle was concerned, we have fortunately since met him at a book signing in Cheltenham.

I recently showed my six and seven-year-old grandchildren, Charlie and Isabelle, all my old climbing paraphernalia, and we had great fun belaying ourselves to bookcases. Then the other morning I looked out of the bedroom window and saw snow on the top of the nearby Cleeve Hill. There seemed to be a finger beckoning once again...